E. Frazer Blackstock

The Land of the Viking and the Empire of the Tsar

E. Frazer Blackstock

The Land of the Viking and the Empire of the Tsar

ISBN/EAN: 9783337170783

Printed in Europe, USA, Canada, Australia, Japan

Cover: Foto ©ninafisch / pixelio.de

More available books at **www.hansebooks.com**

LAPLANDER.

THE
LAND OF THE VIKING

AND THE

EMPIRE OF THE TSAR

BY

E. FRAZER BLACKSTOCK

ILLUSTRATED

NEW YORK AND LONDON
G. P. PUTNAM'S SONS
The Knickerbocker Press
1889

COPYRIGHT BY
E. FRAZER BLACKSTOCK
1889

The Knickerbocker Press
Electrotyped and Printed by
G. P. Putnam's Sons

CONTENTS.

CHAPTER		PAGE
I.	INTO A STRANGE COUNTRY	3
II.	FROM THE NORTH CAPE TO CHRISTIANIA	28
III.	STOCKHOLM EN FÊTE—OVER THE BALTIC	42
IV.	THE GREAT CATHEDRAL — ITS MUSIC, WORSHIPPERS, IKONS, AND STRANGE CEREMONIALS	66
V.	MORE CHURCHES, SHRINES, AND MONASTERIES—DRIVES ABOUT THE CAPITAL	82
VI.	DAYS AT TSARSKOE SELO AND PETERHOF	101
VII.	A GLIMPSE AT THE HERMITAGE	126
VIII.	OUR LAST DAY IN ST. PETERSBURG — SEEING THE WINTER PALACE—ON TO MOSCOW	149
IX.	THE WONDERS OF THE KREMLIN	166
X.	SIGHTS OUTSIDE THE KREMLIN—ADIEU TO RUSSIA	186

LIST OF ILLUSTRATIONS.

	PAGE
LAPLANDER	*Frontispiece*
NORWEGIAN CARRIOLE	10
LAPLANDER'S HUT, NEAR TROMSO	26
THE OLD VIKING SHIP, CHRISTIANIA	38
ST. ISAAC'S CATHEDRAL ST. PETERSBURG	66
EMPEROR OF RUSSIA	100
EMPRESS OF RUSSIA	126
"TSAR-KOLOKOL," OR KING OF BELLS, KREMLIN, MOSCOW	180
CHURCH OF ST. BASIL THE BEATIFIED, MOSCOW	192
ROMANOFF HOUSE, MOSCOW	200

THE LAND OF THE VIKING
AND THE EMPIRE OF
THE TSAR.

DRAMATIS PERSONÆ.

THE CHIEF—*Whose letters to the press won golden opinions, and whose courage surmounted all difficulties.*

THE MATRON—*Whose thoughtful kindness knew no bounds, and who became an experienced whip, overcoming timidity by determination.*

THE SIGNORINA—*The calm, experienced traveller, whose success as a linguist brought joy to our perturbed spirits.*

THE MADAME—*Willing to try all languages and every national dish.*

THE SQUIRE—*Always ready, and of an undaunted spirit.*

THE LAND OF THE VIKING AND THE EMPIRE OF THE TSAR.

CHAPTER I.

INTO A STRANGE COUNTRY.

WITH the first glimpse of the Norwegian coast we felt an instinctive desire to cast ourselves upon the rocks and cling to them, for they at least had an anchorage and were quiet. Oh! that never-to-be-forgotten passage across the North Sea!!!

Sailing up the channel, before reaching Bergen we were charmed with the beauty of earth, sea, and sky. Around us irregular cliffs on either side, dotted here and there with small hamlets, gave us an idea of the thrift of the people. They make the best of every thing. Wherever there is a comparatively level space, some sturdy Norseman has built his little house, and every inch of productive ground is utilized.

We found Bergen a picturesque town of great age, built in the form of a crescent at the foot of a range of hills. The approach is beautiful. The oldest part of the town is on the north side of the harbor, where formerly merchants of the Hanseatic league carried on their business. Now it is the fish-market, and in summer presents a lively appearance. From the deck of our ship we watched men and women preparing the cargoes for numerous small sailing-vessels lying at the wharves. Tons of dried fish were tied into bundles, to be shipped to Rome for use during Lent. How strange the town appeared, with its narrow streets, slanting roofs, quaint old buildings, and appalling hills. From every side came row-boats to meet our ship, and passengers, with their luggage, were conveyed by them to different parts of the town. We drove over a steep, winding road to the Hotel Scandinavie, a quaint, cleanly little hotel, deservedly recommended by Baedeker, where every thing seemed novel to us. We were amused to see our names written in full on a blackboard hanging in the main hall, the number of the room assigned to each guest being placed before the name, an arrangement we found in every hotel in Norway, Sweden, Russia, and Poland.

Our first Norwegian meal was somewhat surprising. The food was clean and well served, but much of it unlike any we had before tasted. Of course there is an abundance of fresh fish. Of the various kinds of bread, only one was palatable. The national *flat-brod*, except for the purpose of experimenting, we left for the natives. The staple article of diet, however, is cheese, there rarely being less than seven varieties at each meal. One resembled a brick in form and color, and the taste must be an acquired one, for it is peculiar, to say the least. " I like cheese," said our Chief, with his characteristic bravery, and with a feeling of anxiety we watched him follow the Norwegian custom of eating some at each meal, experimenting on the seven kinds before leaving Bergen.

From the hour of our arrival we felt a sense of the rest and quiet peculiar to the country. Norwegians seem to be imbued with the idea that life is too precious to rush through, and they spend some hours each day in recreation, banks and offices being closed from twelve to three or thereabouts.

Driving through the town, the pavements were sufficiently bad to remind us of home, but the narrow streets thronged with peasants in national costumes, shops displaying all sorts of wares, and a general primitive air made Bergen attractive to us.

Our first Norwegian sunset we viewed from the summit of a hill adjacent to the hotel. The clouds were of a lovely tint, and the surrounding country bathed in glorious light. It seemed strange to see the ladies with open parasols at ten in the evening. Some children playing on the hill were interested in our enthusiastic appreciation of the view. One of our party, with signs and attempts at Norwegian, tried to induce them to sing some national airs, but failed until copper coins were produced, when they danced and sang vigorously, following us back to the hotel, their big wooden shoes making a great clatter on the sidewalk. The continuous twilight, added to feather beds and eider-down quilts, made sleep almost an impossibility, and one could read all night without artificial light. We heard of a fair American who called for a light to heat her curling-tongs, but none could be found in the hotel, the use of candles and lamps being relegated to the winter months. Alas! for bangs.

The shops occupied our attention one morning, the furriers' and jewelers' wares being tempting. Fine large polar-bear rugs, with stuffed heads, were inexpensive, as also were those of squirrel tails, soft and pretty, whole robes of eider-duck feathers exquisitely dainty but perishable. The silversmith's work is peculiarly fine, and the designs good. For modern articles the prices are reasonable, but all antique silver is most expensive; tankards, cups, spoons, and other articles bought by the jewellers from peasants in the interior of the country are for sale in the shops; queer, short-handled spoons, with round, shallow bowls, have grotesque designs engraved upon them. The fine old *répousée* tankards are suggestive of the capacity of former generations for imbibing the delicious Norwegian ale. The modern gold, silver, and oxidized filagree jewelry and articles of carved wood are purchased in quantities by travellers.

Oh! that *carriole* drive which, through the brilliantly sarcastic letter of our Chief, has become historic. He was importuned to accompany us, but firmly declined, realizing, I suppose, how much more enjoyment could be derived from jeering at the rest of us on our return, which he did without mercy. To describe our start is beyond the power of my pen, but a slight idea of the procession can be had by imagining four *carrioles* (like the sketch) in a line, with a small boy on the back of the last one. The floor being small, the Madame's feet had to ride outside, which was restful if not picturesque. The Squire led off in great style, followed by the Matron, pale and determined, clutching with vigor the cords which served as reins; next the Signorina, calm and unconcerned, with the air of one who had often been there before; lastly the Madame, with the worst horse in the crowd; however, he came in first. The excitement in Bergen became intense, the small boys congregating in such numbers that a policeman was forced to disperse the crowd.

NORWEGIAN CARRIOLE.

How the sturdy Norwegian ponies did go up hill and down without a break, the springless *carrioles* jolting the drivers to an exhausting degree!

The country about Bergen is beautiful, and the roads excellent. Driving along the base of a mountain we saw many houses in apparently inaccessible spots; it seems as if some of the picturesque *châlets* might drop down from their lofty elevation, built as they were on narrow ledges. The haymakers were working busily in the fields, and many stopped to gaze after the cavalcade dashing by. The women far outnumbered the men; many of them had their little children playing in the fresh sweet-smelling hay, and babies lay basking in the glorious sunlight. Peasants, policemen, patricians, plebeians, all had a pleasant greeting for us.

About one Norwegian, or seven English miles, from Bergen stands the summer residence of the United States Consul, where an old stone church, found in the interior, was brought in sections and erected in the beautiful park, where it is an object of interest to the tourist, not having been used for service for hundreds of years. It resembles a Chinese pagoda, and is supposed to have been built in the eleventh century; the grotesque paintings on the walls represent different saints, the colors being well preserved. As we stood by the altar I could not help wondering what manner of people worshipped there so long, long ago; how little we knew of them; their existence seems almost mythical.

On an island not far from Bergen is the country home of the late Ole Bull. His memory is dear to the people of his country, and also to us who were privileged to hear him play with the rare expression and brilliant execution peculiar to himself. The famous composer, Edward Grieg, also lives in Bergen, and having seen the picturesque country I can believe that he draws inspiration for his lovely music from his surroundings. In the interesting and complete natural-history collection is the largest whale skeleton in Europe. In the same museum we also saw several old church portals, curiously carved, brought from the Sognedal valley, some music ornaments, a large number of antique tankards, cabinets, wardrobes, and beds; one of the latter, being elaborately carved, is probably of Dutch workmanship. From the top of the Rosencrantz tower, now used as an arsenal, we had a fine view.

An event worthy of more than a passing allusion was a business arrangement which introduced to us a young Norseman who impressed us greatly. He was tall, well built, fair-haired, blue-eyed, and seemed to be a descendant of some old Viking, possibly the one said to have built for his lovely bride a stone habitation on these shores centuries before the authenticated discovery of America, and whose "lofty tower still to this very hour stands looking seaward." In his strength and beauty the "Modern Viking," as the Signorina dubbed him, seemed a splendid specimen of the highest type of Scandinavian civilization. The last time we saw him we were overpowered by his majesty and might; the very air surrounding him seemed impregnated with an aroma of wassail-bowls, feasts, and junketings of bygone days, and we almost expected him to raise a tankard to his lips, crying: "Skoal! to the Norseman Skoal!" but as he drew nearer the indefinable something became a well-defined odor of garlic and onions!! Alas! our Viking was human and had lunched. We transacted our business hastily and fled.

We saw many things of interest and much that was novel. While there were few evidences of great wealth, there seemed to be very little extreme poverty, and the people are good-humored and contented. We started for Throndhjem and the North Cape on Friday evening by the *Olaf Kyrre* of the Det Bergensk Nordland Skeselskab, a formidable name for a line of steamers, but a model company for all that, as we were surprised to find the boat equal to the best transatlantic steamers. The Signorina and the Madame being lucky in occupying the captain's large and luxurious cabin on deck, afternoon tea soon became the rule.

During the thirty-eight-hour trip

to Throndhjem we passed through magnificent scenery; the irregular snow-capped mountains were about us continually; the channel wound in and out among myriads of islands, and the sea was as smooth as the proverbial mill-pond. At each stopping place row-boats came out to meet the steamer for the purpose of conveying passengers to and fro. At Molde, the entrance to the Romsdal, the beauty of earth, sea, and sky was transcendent. Leaving Christiansund shortly before ten on Saturday evening, we had a vision of the New Jerusalem—the different tints on the hill's snowy peaks, peaceful sea, together with the sun sinking into the waters, shedding the most exquisite light, left an impression that can never be effaced. If in this sin-cursed world such beauty exists, what must be the glory beyond the clouds! The veil that separates us from Heaven seemed very thin to us then, and we almost felt as if we were standing before the Throne. The rules of the steamship company forbid passengers remaining on board while at Throndhjem, where we arrived early Sunday morning. The Hotel Angleterre, patronized by Cook's tourists, we found noisy and untidy; card-playing and drinking in all the public rooms forced the English and American travellers to remain in their apartments while in the hotel.

We attended service in the picturesque stone chapter-house belonging to the cathedral built in 1100 by King Olaf Kyrre. It is an imposing structure, having a subterranean passage to an island in the harbor, which was used in by-gone days as a means of escape from justice. The holy well of St. Olaf and a fine copy of Thorwaldsen's celebrated statue of Christ are the principal objects of interest. The king of Sweden and Norway, after his coronation in Stockholm, comes to Throndhjem to be crowned in the chancel of this cathedral. During the summer English service is conducted in the chapter-house, there always being a large number of tourists in town.

Throndhjem is busy and prosperous, but there is little to see, although some of our party found the leper hospital worth visiting. What misery, suffering, and wretchedness are suggested by the name of that loathsome disease; during its early stages the mind of the afflicted one must be a prey to the most hopeless despair beyond human aid; there is nothing to anticipate in this life but repulsive and gradual physical and mental decay; only a firm faith in God and a hope of dwelling hereafter with Him who, when on earth, cleansed the lepers from their dreadful taint, will help them endure to the bitter end all the horror of their lot. Strange to say, in spite of the pure air of Norway, there is much of the disease in the country.

On Monday evening we started for the North Cape in good earnest. The steamer was comfortably filled with about one hundred passengers. When we went on board we were greeted as old friends by the captain and officers. Most of the inhabitants of Throndhjem assembled to see the steamer off, and a brass band on the quay played various national airs. Altogether it was a lively scene, and the peasants in their gay costumes, with variegated kerchiefs on the women's heads, made a bit of bright color in the landscape. Many countries were represented among the passengers: a large party of Parisians, one of Germans, some Hungarians, and a few Scandinavians were hilarious. The English-speaking tourists had a private table in the ladies' cabin, thanks to the thoughtful kindness of Captain Getz, who realized that mingling with so many foreigners would be uncongenial. Breakfast, at nine o'clock, consisted of tea, coffee, several varieties of fish, one dish of meat, and the seven ubiquitous cheeses. Supper, at eight o'clock, was a similar meal, but the event of the day was an elaborate, well-served dinner at three o'clock, after which we had coffee on deck *en famille*. Notwithstanding all that tourists have said and written to the contrary, we found the food abundant and very palatable.

Among the English-speaking travellers, we had, of course, a bride and groom, whose ecstasies over each other were greater than when passing

Into a Strange Country. 21

through the most sublime scenery. "But," said the Chief, with his usual charity, "forgive them, they are so happy, so oblivious to all the world, and remember that it cannot last." Also the flirtatious American whose steamer-chair was surrounded by admirers, and who said, with mild enthusiasm, when the first glory of the midnight sun burst upon us: "Is n't that real pretty, Mr. S. Don't you think a gown like the pink tint on that mountain would be just too sweet for any thing?" "Yes," he replied in a low tone and with an ardent look; "and it would just match the color in your cheeks and ——" Waiting to hear no more, I fled precipitately to the captain's bridge, not being able to enjoy the similarity between midnight suns and cheeks.

Two sisters and a brother (English) did every thing in the most approved guide-book style—alpenstocks, boots, gaiters, marine-glasses, and caps, all new-purchased for the trip; profuse notes of travel copied verbatim from Baedeker, and a continual "Aw! this is awfully jolly, don't-cher-know; perfect education for a fellah; but what a beastly bore to meet so many Yankees! they're goin' all over the world now, don't-cher-know, they are so beastly rich," and so forth *ad nauseam.* Alas! for us, the musical amateurs were there in numbers, and at their concert (heaven save the mark!) they rendered one of the most glorious nights hideous. A romance of short duration was the mutual admiration of the good-looking second-officer and a pretty, fair-haired fraulein, who fancied no lookers-on noticed their coy blushes and loving glances. Alas! there was no moonlight for them, and love-making in the sun had always seemed an im-

Into a Strange Country. 23

possibility until we saw how successful they were.

Every hour the scenery became finer, the Norwegian coast being remarkably diversified. On Tuesday we dropped anchor at the famous Torghaetten Rock, and after a long, fatiguing climb we reached the point where there is a fine view through the "hole in the hat," which is the literal meaning of the name. A large opening in the mountain gave a beautiful panorama of the sea and adjacent islands. According to the legend, a giantess pursued by an importunate lover was saved by an arrow from her brother's bow piercing the hat and head of her pursuer, hence the name. The climb was doubly difficult on account of the intense heat. At intervals, on the winding, stony path, we found peasants offering fresh milk for sale, which was very acceptable, and they were grateful for the few copper coins given them.

The evenings or rather nights, on deck were glorious; watching the sun set at half-past ten and rise again shortly after one was an uncanny experience; the golden clouds and different tints on the mountains—orange, pink, and purple—were indescribably beautiful. The sail through the picturesque Lofoden islands was one of the most enjoyable experiences of the trip; at times the channel was so narrow that it seemed impossible for the steamer to avoid running against the rugged cliffs; again one would fancy that there was no outlet for us, so surrounded were we by the "everlasting hills," that to turn about would be the only way to solve the problem. We passed quite near the Maelstrom, the danger of which is much less than has been popularly supposed. What recollections of school-days it revived; how vague one's childish ideas were as to what the Maelstrom really was! It seemed as if in the seething fury of the waves there was a cruel, relentless fiend grasping all within reach, and dragging down to a horrible death brave sailors, whose struggles to escape were futile; but, although the current is very swift, with strong power of suction, there are few instances of boats being lost.

Passing the far-famed Seven Sisters, we found them seven cliffs of striking uniformity, side by side. After entering the Arctic Circle we noticed in certain places in the water a beautiful, transparent, grass-green hue, said to be caused by the innumerable *ctenophora* which it contains, and these frolicsome microscopic creatures are also phosphorescent. Huge glaciers, green fields, rugged mountains, combined with the novelty of sailing in the Arctic Ocean, overwhelmed us, and when we had the first sight of the midnight sun in all its majestic splendor, we felt that the acme of wonder was reached; the exquisite sunsets of the previous nights were but a preparation for the glories we were privileged to see later. The weather was fine, and one felt that each moment spent in eating and sleeping was wasted; nevertheless, we continued our meals with striking regularity.

At Tromso a Lapp encampment was the attraction, and the diminutive, fur-clad, wretchedly dirty people seemed less like human beings than animals. The tribe is a large one, and well off as Lapps go; they have a fine herd of reindeer, and all seem to live together. Many passengers bought souvenirs from the women and children, but they were too dirty for me to go sufficiently near to make

LAPLANDER'S HUT, NEAR TROMSO.

purchases. After visiting the encampment, we wandered about Tromso, a straggling town, but of course boasting of several fur shops. At dinner we were served with reindeer tongues, as a reminder of the Lapps, I suppose, and they were most palatable.

At Hammerfest, the most northern town in Europe, letters and cablegrams were sent by all the passengers, and a thriving business in stamps was done at the post. It is a compact, well-built little town, the inhabitants making their living by fishing; the wharfs are lined with small sailing-boats, and the air is strongly impregnated with fish oil. We remained on deck nearly all night, not wishing to lose the glorious effect of sun and clouds at twelve o'clock. When the cannon was fired an enterprising Norwegian photographer took a group of passengers by the strong light of the sun.

CHAPTER II.

FROM THE NORTH CAPE TO CHRISTIANIA.

THE goal of our ambition was reached on Friday evening; anchoring two hundred yards from the shore, the passengers were rowed in small boats to the landing-stage at the foot of the North Cape. Having waited until all the foreigners had started, we went on shore at ten o'clock and the ascent began. Ye gods! what a climb it was; it reminded us of childhood's one step forward and two steps back; for some fifty yards we had to scramble over stones and rocks, there being no path. When a third of the distance had been accomplished, we came upon a strong rope fastened to iron posts, which was of great assistance; after that the sensation was extremely like walking up the side of a house, the narrow zigzag path being worn perfectly smooth by a multitude of tourists.

An hour's climbing brought us to the summit, and then, after a walk of a mile over the plateau, we reached the place where the finest view was to be had. Separating ourselves from the crowd, we went off to a lonely promontory where we could quietly enjoy the wonderful experience. Although obscured by clouds, the sun cast the most exquisite shades on sea and mountains, and a peculiar pink tint on a rugged cliff toward the south was indescribably beautiful. There on the summit of the North Cape looking over the vast expanse of the Arctic Ocean, a feeling of profound awe filled our hearts, and the solemn memory of that hour will always be a cherished one. The weather being mild, it was difficult to realize that we were so far north, and we felt a strong inclination to sail farther and farther into the arctic regions. The weird desolation of the scene was intensified by the utter absence of all animal life. Gazing into the infinite space, we seemed alone with Deity; a strong realization of our own insignificance forced itself upon us, and our souls were filled with reverence and adoration for the Almighty Creator of the universe. The strangely powerful influence that nature exerts over human beings was never more potent than when we stood upon the North Cape.

Meanwhile, at the point, the foreigners were drinking, dancing, and singing (?) to the accompaniment of an execrable brass band which boarded the *Olaf Kyrre* at Hammerfest, and played at the most inopportune hours. A fine granite monument in memory of King Oscar's visit in 1873 has been erected on the Point. The descent was, if possible, worse than the ascent; the sensation was like skating down a toboggan slide. There, on the summit and sides of the North Cape, are ferns, buttercups, forget-me-nots, and many varieties of wild flowers growing in profusion.

After returning to the ship, most of the passengers commenced fishing, and over one hundred cod were caught in less than an hour. Five o'clock tea at two A.M. was very refreshing, most of us being too excited to sleep. Walking the deck until six o'clock gave opportunity for talking over the wonders of the North Cape. We were so glad to have taken the trip, in spite of much advice to the contrary, several friends having told us that it was not worth the time and trouble; but to us the experience was of the greatest interest and pleasure, and one that would bear an early repetition.

One of the largest glaciers in Europe the Svartisen, was reached on Saturday. Many passengers went ashore and wandered about, looking for bears, and finding bluebells. The same afternoon we saw the famous bird-rock, one of the sights of Norway: a high rugged cliff was entirely covered with row upon row of small gulls; the rock seemed to be a succession of ledges, where the birds were perched in strange regularity. At the firing of one of the ship's cannon, myriads flew upward, completely obscuring the sky for nearly a minute, then settled down again on the rock, to await another startling cannon. While flying upward, the effect was very peculiar, and they uttered a strange, hoarse cry.

The entire distance from the North Cape back to Throndhjem was a succession of beautiful sights; the Lyngenfiord, where we sailed for a day, is specially picturesque, and comparatively little known, on account of being so far north; only tourists going to the cape have the pleasure of seeing it. On Saturday night we had the finest view of the midnight sun, and were overpowered at the transcendent beauty of the sight. The sun was a ball of fire, and the surrounding clouds ranging in color from red to palest pink. Although extremely cold a privileged few remained on the captain's bridge until three A.M., enjoying every moment of the wondrous vision. Our chief conducted service on Sunday, which was attended by a majority of the passengers, and we spent a peaceful, quiet day amidst beautiful scenery.

Before leaving the ship, some resolutions were drafted, signed by all the passengers, referring in the highest terms to the ability, courtesy, and thoughtfulness of Captain Getz and his subordinates. After reading them, our chief called for cheers, which were heartily given and modestly acknowledged by the officers. I can only advise any reader who contemplates taking this trip, to endeavor to secure passage by the *Olaf Kyrre*, which for comfort and cleanliness is a model steamer.

We reached Throndhjem on Monday morning, and after saying goodbye to our fellow passengers we went to the Hotel Nordkap to rest for a few hours before starting for Christiania. It seems to me that the beauty of Norway must inspire the inhabitants to noble deeds and purity of life, for who could be mean or base living in a country where the scenery is so grand and majestic. One cannot help being selfish enough to regret that every year the number of tourists visiting Norway is increasing; it would be a thousand pities to have that picturesque country desecrated by the average sight-seers, as so many others have been, and this feeling makes one desirous of seeing it thoroughly before the aggressive tourists have succeeded in robbing it of its primitive charm.

We left Throndhjem for Christiania in a sleeper, so called, but it was a most uncomfortable railway carriage. When pulled out to serve as beds the springless seats were not luxurious, no mattresses being furnished, and only a coarse, gray blanket for bedding. We felt little inclination to sleep, but discomfort was soon forgotten in the beauty of the country, and we spent the greater part of the night looking out of the windows. For some distance the railroad skirts

Lake Myosen, the largest and one of the most picturesque lakes in Norway. Meals at the Norwegian railway-stations are strangely conducted; in the middle of the dining-room stands a large table covered with hot and cold dishes, plates, knives, forks, condiments, and an infinite variety of cheese. Each person appropriates a plate, knife, and fork, places it on a table prepared only with a spotlessly clean cloth, turns up a chair to indicate the place to be occupied, and going to a table in the corner of the room receives a cup of tea or coffee. It is an easy matter to go away without paying for one's meal, there being no attendants except at the coffee-table, and Norwegians expect strangers to be as honest as themselves, which is certainly saying a great deal.

Christiania, the capital of Norway, with a population of over one hundred

North Cape to Christiania. 37

and twenty thousand, is beautifully situated at the north end of the Christiania fiord. There seems to be a great deal of wealth in the city, many of the houses being large and luxurious. We found the well appointed Victoria Hotel comfortable in every respect; the elaborate *table d'hôte* dinner was served at three o'clock in a gayly decorated tent erected in the court, where tables and chairs were scattered about for smoking and drinking coffee after the meal. Parliament buildings, university, museum of art, and palace are well-built, imposing structures, the latter being surrounded by beautiful gardens open to the public.

Driving about the city was very enjoyable, the pavements being excellent, the streets wide and clean. From St. John's Hill the view of a picturesque country is fine. A short distance from the city stands the chateau of Oscarshall, built on a cliff overlooking the fiord; its situation is beautiful. Being merely used as an occasional resort on summer afternoons by the royal family, we had no difficulty in seeing the whole villa, which contains much of interest. The state dining-room, a charming apartment, is filled with pictures by eminent native artists; ten by Tidemand represent different phases of Norwegian peasant life. Rooms on the second-floor contain numerous gifts to King Oscar from different monarchs; also some of his majesty's uniforms and the gorgeously ugly coronation robes of the present queen and her predecessor. There is a charming view of the city fiord and environs from the top of the tower.

In a shed behind the university stands the old Viking ship discovered in a mound some eight years since. Similar in shape to the Norwegian

fishing-boat of the present time, it is built of oak, now jet black, is in a good state of preservation, and it is wellnigh impossible to believe that its age is nearly one thousand years. One peculiarity is the rudder at the side; the bolts used in its construction are like those used in these days. The bones of the Viking, with those of his favorite dogs and horses, were found in the sepulchral chamber in the middle of the ship, together with many ornaments and cooking utensils, all buried together in the ninth century, presumably. That wonderful craft! Standing beside it gave one a strange sensation: how old it was; what changes had been wrought in the world's history during the centuries it lay buried. The remains of the Viking proved him to have been a large, muscular, fair man; what could have been his life? he was without doubt brave and daring;

perchance the Norse prince, Leif, was of his family,—that prince who is said to have reached Mt. Hope Bay, Massachusetts, hundreds of years before Columbus sailed westward. Had he dear ones who mourned his death ; or did he sever all his ties of blood and affection when he joined the rovers of the seas. Is it possible that the Vikings were human like ourselves ? To us they seem mystical and unreal, but of great interest. It was late in the day when we went to see the old ship, and in the dim light it almost seemed like some relic of another world, so weird and uncanny it looked, and every-day life with eating and drinking was far from our thoughts.

Reflecting upon the pleasant days spent in Norway, I begin to realize what a pleasure and privilege it was to see a little of that picturesque and restful country, where life presents so striking a contrast to the hurry and bustle of America. Can a greater difference be imagined than that between the slow, easy, trustful existence of the average Norseman, and the rapid, unrestful struggle of the people on this side of the Atlantic? A summer spent in Norway is a great boon to a busy man burdened with cares and responsibilities, for it is impossible to help resting mentally and physically, as in the very air of the country there is a sense of peace and repose. The people have always a warm welome for strangers; their lives are simple and wholesome, and their love of country very strong. A short and hurried trip, as ours necessarily was, made us desirous of returning soon, and driving through the country, taking it slowly, and seeing much of peasant life. It is an excellent country to economize in; hotel charges are moderate; driving inexpensive; and a small tip thankfully received.

CHAPTER III.

STOCKHOLM EN FÊTE—OVER THE BALTIC.

A SECOND night in a Norwegian sleeper, an improvement upon the first, brought us to Stockholm, the Swedish capital. Built upon Lake Malaren, the situation of the city, surrounded by islands and water in every direction, is exceeding picturesque; and Stockholm is justly called "the Venice of the North." On approaching we found that the city was *en fête:* flags, arches, decorations everywhere, in honor of the Kaiser's visit, who, with his suite, was spending two days at the Swedish capital *en route* from St. Petersburg to Denmark.

The large and elegantly appointed Grand Hotel has a fine situation, commanding a view of the busy harbor, and is quite near the National Museum, where the royal family was paying a visit when we arrived from the railway station. The head-waiter gave us a window in the salon, where we had an excellent view of the street, crowded with expectant people watching for the royal party returning to the Schloss. We considered ourselves fortunate in receiving a special salute from King Oscar II. and the Kaiser, as they drove past, followed by many notable persons, among them Prince Heinrich of Prussia, Count Herbert Bismarck, and a large retinue of German and Swedish officers. The good-looking young Emperor had a very bored expression, not a muscle of his face relaxing at the enthusiastic cheers of the people. King Oscar is a remarkably handsome and genial-looking man, and every inch a king. As the royal people were driving about the city most of the day, we saw them several times. At noon there was a great booming of cannon, and flags were run up in every possible place on the German yachts to celebrate the birth of a son to the Empress at Potsdam.

The squadron commanded by Prince Heinrich, brother of the Kaiser, was anchored in the harbor some two miles from the city, and the ten gayly decorated ships presented a fine appearance. From the roof of the hotel we watched the departure of the royal visitor and his suite after saying adieu to King Oscar on the elaborate landing-stage. One by one they stepped into small boats, each manned by twelve seamen in the uniform of the royal middies, and were rowed to the yachts amid the booming of cannon, cheers of the people, and bands playing.

Stockholm has great natural advantages; being intersected by canals, it is customary to pass from one part of the city to another by means of the innumerable small steam launches plying in every direction. Swedish girls, in picturesque national costumes, row about in well appointed skiffs, their charges for passengers being merely nominal. The people of Stockholm live much out-of-doors; numerous restaurants and gardens being filled with pleasure-seekers, drinking beer or coffee, and listening to excellent music, which can always be heard in the evenings. The Swedes impressed us as being an intelligent, patriotic, prosperous, and contented people, and they are by far the best class of immigrants coming to America, being thrifty and conscientious.

The royal family is one of the most popular and beloved in Europe; the king and queen are very democratic, driving about and receiving visitors in an unostentatious way. Their second son, Prince Oscar, recently married Miss Munck, a beautiful woman in attendance upon the queen, and by so doing relinquished his claim to the throne; the third son, Prince Carl, one of the handsomest men in Europe, is in the army.

Most of the buildings in Stockholm are large and imposing; the National Museum, a building in the Renaissance style, is filled with interesting collections of pictures, statuary, coins, ecclesiastical furniture, and Egyptian articles. The colossal marble statues, in the vestibule, of Odin, Thor, and Baldur, the Scandinavian divinities, were suggestive of the fascinating mythology of school-days. The large collection of antiquities consists of articles for domestic use, ornaments and implements of all kinds belonging to the flint, bronze, and iron periods, many having been discovered in ancient tombs, where they had so long lain buried. The gem of the sculpture is a parian sleeping " Endymion " excavated in the last century at Hadrian's Villa Tivoli. The perfect repose of the exquisite figure fills one with a sense of rest, and in its naturalness it almost seems to breathe. Among the hundreds of pictures are many of great merit, and nearly all the old masters are well represented ; Rembrandt's " Oath of Ziska " is very fine, and, although unfinished, is one of his greatest works. On the lawn on the northwest side of the museum stands the " Girdle Duellists," a fine bronze group by Mulin, which interested me very much, not only for its intrinsic worth as a work of art, but also on account of the strange custom it represents. In the olden days the Scandinavians were bound together by belts, and so fought out their duels with murderous-looking knives. The people being very hot-headed, quarrels were easily provoked, and it is said that women used to carry winding sheets for their husbands to banquets where differences were likely to arise, as the contest always ended fatally to one or both duellists, and under such circumstances the feast could not have been altogether enjoyable to the wives.

In the Northern Museum is a large and interesting Scandinavia collection; the women attendants are dressed in the picturesque Darlecarlia costumes, and there one can form a fairly accurate idea of Swedish life from groups of wax figures, with appropriate surroundings, representing different scenes in peasant homes.

The large square palace standing on a rocky elevation, commands a fine view of the canals and harbor. Of course, like all other palaces, it contains much of interest; and the state apartments are fine, of which the large banqueting-room, the "Hvita Hafvet," or the White Sea, finished in white stucco, and furnished appropriately, is the most imposing. The private apartments of the royal family were shown, and the greatest liberty was accorded us; sitting by the king's writing-table, and in his Majesty's chair, we had quite a feeling of "being to the manner born," as it were. The suite occupied by the Kaiser during his visit had evidently been newly furnished for the occasion, much of the hangings and furniture coverings being a brilliant green; we thought the effect on the imperial complexion must have been somewhat trying. Counected with

King Oscar's smoking-room is a small glass apartment used as a winter parlor, having a profusion of vines growing on the walls and being furnished with excellent taste; it is a cheerful and home-like nook, and we were told by the lackey that it was a favorite sitting-room of the royal family.

Scattered about the palace are many beautiful ornaments presented to King Oscar by different monarchs, and also by his loyal subjects; and a profusion of embroidery and painted work, done by the skilful members of the Bernadotte family. All the Swedes we had the pleasure of meeting spoke in terms of the highest regard of the King and Queen and their children; they do much good among the poor, and take a deep interest in the welfare of their subjects. Among the numerous churches, the "Riddarholms Kyrka" is the most interesting; for centuries it has been the burial-place of Sweden's kings and most celebrated men; for many years no services have been held in it, except on the occasion of royal funerals.

After a fatiguing day of sight-seeing we enjoyed a drive in the " Djurgarden," a beautiful park laid out on an island a short distance from the city, and of which the people of Stockholm are justly proud. " Rosendal," a large villa built by Charles XIV. John, with extensive hot-houses and orangeries, is well situated near the water. Not far distant is a statue to the memory of the great poet and improvisatore, Karl Michael Bellman, some of whose most charming ballads were composed under the shade of an adjacent oak; many of his best poems were made *extempore*, and with perfect ease. Stockholm's finest restaurant is in the " Djur-garden," and the

"Hasselbacken" is famous for its fine situation, excellent cuisine, and magnificent orchestra, and in fine weather is always well patronized.

The pleasure of our visit to Stockholm was greatly enhanced by the kindness of some charming Swedish friends of our chief, to whose thoughtful attention the greater part of our enjoyment was due. We accompanied them to the summer palace of Drottningholm, situated on the most beautiful of Lake Malaren's numerous islands, about seven miles from the city, and during the charming sail thither we passed many summer residences of wealthy city people. The famous architect, Nicodemus Tessin, designed the beautiful palace, which is sumptuously fitted up and perfect in all its details; it contains a large number of pictures and other works of art, and the home-like private rooms were most attractive. The extensive grounds are laid out in imitation of those at Versailles, and the fine fountains play frequently in summer. A Chinese pagoda is a curious little building, and the details well carried out.

A few days previously a large luncheon party had been given in honor of the Kaiser in the great banqueting-room, and before leaving the palace his Majesty had written his name in the visitors' book (and written it well, too); and, of course, we had the honor of sitting at the same table and in the same chair while inscribing our names in the precious volume. Drottningholm is the favorite residence of the royal family, and we could easily understand the charm this beautiful and tranquil place has for the privileged few residing there. A dinner-party drive to "Hasselbacken," where we greatly enjoyed the fine music, and a moonlight sail back to the hotel made our last day in Stockholm very enjoyable. The great kindness shown us by our Swedish friends was almost overpowering, and after making our visit delightful in every way, they started us off for St. Petersburg with the kindest of adieus, and laden with flowers and bon-bons.

Well-built, well-paved, and scrupulously clean, Stockholm impressed us as being a model city, and we wished that on this side of the Atlantic the civic authorities would strive for the degree of perfection the "Venice of the North" seems to have attained. The numerous lines of street railways are well managed; the civil conductors and drivers wearing neat and appropriate uniforms; the large, comfortable cars are very clean; and the drivers have the rare faculty of stopping the horses so that the rear platform is on the crossing.

I was much impressed while in Norway and Sweden with the striking contrast between these Protestant countries and those where Catholicism holds sway; there is no abject poverty, and one is never importuned by beggars, as in Italy, for example; the people work in a contented way, do the best they can, and enjoy the results of their labor in a rational manner.

Across the Baltic we started for St. Petersburg, expectant and full of excitement. It seemed strange that we were really to go to Russia, that remarkable country, which has so much prominence in modern thought, writing, and discussions. Our ideas were chaotic, and we felt that in going there we took our lives in our hands, but continued to go as fast as the good steamer would take us.

Finland! The name suggests a

barren, uncivilized country, peopled by creatures after the order of Lapps. Our preconceived ideas were wrong, and on reaching Helsingfors, the capital of the Grand Duchy of Finland, we found it a large, well built, imposing city, with a population of 50,000, having a university, museum, palace, fine theatre, numerous churches, and a large park. The new hotel on the esplanade proved even better than the Grand in Stockholm, and there we enjoyed our first Russian meal before continuing our journey to St. Petersburg. In the evening the park was filled with Finns, walking about, drinking *vodki*, and listening to an excellent orchestra, apparently enjoying civilization, and conducting themselves very much like any other people.

Passing Cronstadt we found the extensive fortifications of great strength; from there we sailed up the narrow canal, by which all large steamers are obliged to reach St. Petersburg, and which is one of the most remarkable works of the kind in Europe.

Forty hours after leaving Stockholm, the first glimpse of the Russian capital thrilled us all. There, glittering in the sunlight, rose the gilded dome of St. Isaac's, and, drawing nearer and nearer to that wonderful city our excitement increased, and we could not realize that at last we were approaching St. Petersburg. It seemed like a dream, but on reaching the wharf and seeing mighty officials armed with authority to examine all our belongings, and even to prevent us from landing, if they thought fit, we found that we were to deal with stern realities. Looking down from the deck of the steamer we saw a heterogeneous collection of men; custom-house officials in gorgeous green and gold uniforms, looking as if they could be very unpleasant on slight provocation; moujiks waiting to carry luggage to the busses and other vehicles in the street; commissionaires looking for employment; all talking in a language sounding like a cross between Choctaw and Chinese.

The passport and custom-house formalities were soon over, and going through to the street we were met by Pilly, the *valet de place* engaged by us previously. According to the description given of him by our chief, he is the greatest mixture of humility and egotism, knowledge and ignorance, in Europe. He proved himself perfectly invaluable, and Murray's guide-book justly recommends him as the best courier in the country. It is the height of folly to attempt travelling in Russia without an experienced guide; in the matter of hiring a cab, for example, it is necessary to make a bargain; there being no regular tariff, the drosky driver always asks a stranger at least five times more than he expects to receive, and bargaining in English with a Russian is a very hopeless matter for the traveller.

How strange every thing looked to us during the long drive from the wharf to the hotel. Most of the streets seemed deserted, for the city is so vast that the population of nine hundred thousand is not sufficient to fill it, and, except on the Nevski Prospect, there are comparatively few people. Few women are seen walking in public,—in that as in many other respects Russia retains a trace of Orientalism. We passed queer little shops with painted signs on each side of the entrance representing the wares sold inside; butchers, with legs of mutton and impossible-looking poultry; bakeries, with gigantic rolls and loaves too highly colored to tempt one's appetite; boot shops whose strangely shaped gear could not by any stretch of imagination be supposed to fit the human foot; mammoth peaches, oranges, and grapes at the fruiterers, and grotesque costumes of by-gone days at the dry-goods shops; it did not seem possible that we were in Europe, for the gay colors, innumerable domes and minarets, and strange dress of the people make St. Petersburg very Oriental in appearance.

Arriving at the Grand Hotel d'Europe on the Nevski Prospect, we found a huge building of red stucco; a group of moujiks stood on the sidewalk, waiting to help us alight from the omnibus, clothed in long red shirts with crash aprons, trousers tucked into high boots; with their dark heavy faces framed in masses of long straight hair they looked very strange. Before our rooms were assigned our passports were given up and sent to the police to be registered and viséd, so we were under surveillance every moment while in St. Petersburg, as in Moscow and Warsaw. The hotel proved very luxurious; our comfortable rooms on the second floor were moderate in price; the charge for a large salon with two bedrooms adjoining was only six roubles, or three dollars, per day for the Signorina and the Madame; every thing included, our daily hotel bill did not average more than $4.50 each, which seemed reasonable.

The main dining-room, in white and gold with marble floor, is a beautiful apartment; during *table-d'hôte* the English waiter appointed to look after American travellers gave his advice as to our choice of dishes. First comes the " Zakouska," a cold meal of every kind of *hors d'œuvres*, accompanied by *vodki*, the Russian whiskey. One's appetite for dinner is supposed to be heightened by partaking liberally of caviare, raw herring, anchovies, sardines, salads, and various other relishes. Fortunately, although the government is the most despotic in the world, travellers are allowed to use their own discretion as to the amount of food they require. For dinner there are always two soups, one Russian and one civilized; the former, tasting like a combination of equal quantities of sour cream and cabbage, is perfectly cold. The fruit was remarkably good, and the native wines, made in the Crimea, light and palatable. It was a usual thing to see pretty women joining the men at table in an after-dinner smoke; they use a special brand of cigarettes and apparently enjoy it as much as the stronger sex.

In the well appointed reading-room we found, in addition to Russian journals, London and New York papers, in nearly all of which some paragraphs were undecipherable, having been blackened by order of the censor of the press. All newspapers, books, and pamphlets are carefully perused by this powerful official or his subordinates before being delivered to those to whom they are directed, and any article casting reflections upon the government or royal family is promptly obliterated by a roller of black ink being passed over it, and through the black density not a word can be read. In spite of the injustice of this strict law, I could not help wishing that in some way a quietus could be put upon the license of the press on this side of the Atlantic, for there seems to be no limit to the liberty tolerated in the journals of the present day.

After dinner Pilly came to us saying: "Ladies, and gentlemen, and Miss, there is a special service in St. Isaac's this evening, would you not like to hear the music?" It required very little time to prepare for what proved to be a great pleasure, and we were soon driving rapidly down the Nevski Prospect in a landau drawn by a span of powerful black horses, our coachman urging them on with kindly words, terms of endearment, and vigorously cracking his long whip in the air, which, however, never touched the horses. The Russians rarely ill-treat their animals, but talk to them as if they were imbued with human intellect: "Go on, little brother"; "Be quick, my little friend"; "Hurry up, my father," etc., etc. The strange dress of the coachman is the same, whether employed by the nobility or driving the commonest drosky; of course there are degrees of cleanliness and ornamentation, but they all wear long coats reaching to the ground, buttoned diagonally, tied at the waist with an embroidered girdle; this, with an abbreviated bell-crowned beaver hat surmounting a shock of matted hair, gives them a grotesque appearance.

CHAPTER IV.

THE GREAT CATHEDRAL—ITS MUSIC, WORSHIPPERS, IKONS, AND STRANGE CEREMONIALS.

ST. ISAAC'S! What recollections are awakened by the name of the mightiest cathedral of northern Europe! That vast edifice, filled with the choicest products of this world's mines, how it loomed before us, and as we approached we were filled with a sense of our inability to appreciate its vast proportions and superb architecture at a single visit. Built in the form of the Greek cross, with an imposing entrance on each of the four sides, it is approached from the level of the street by broad flights of steps of polished Finnish granite, each flight cut from a single block,

ST. ISAAC'S CATHEDRAL, ST. PETERSBURG.

which required enormous expenditure of money and labor. At each of the entrances are twenty-eight pillars supporting the portico, monoliths of the same rare granite, perfectly round and smooth. Scores of statues and bas-reliefs are of bronze, and the magnificently carved doors are of the same metal. One is perfectly overwhelmed at the magnificence of the exterior, and although service had commenced we lingered outside, loth to enter until we had examined some few of the details.

"Come," said Pilly, "or you'll be pretty sorry if you miss the music, besides its much gorgeouser inside"; and truly he was right. In we went, past the rows of begging nuns who are always to be found at the church doors, being sent out from the convents to raise a certain sum of money; when this is accomplished they return to their several convents and are cared for during the remainder of their lives; but they were so dirty and repulsive, that we felt that if the sum required were a large one they might stand for years before collecting it.

Just within the doors we stopped spell-bound; service was going on and we, with the exception of the Signorina, heard for the first time the wonderful music of the Russo-Greek Church. No instruments being allowed, and the choir being composed of boys and men, their ages ranging from perhaps eight to forty years, the harmonies are sublime, and although there is great repetition in the chanting, it never becomes wearisome; the " Guspodi Guspodi," or " Lord have mercy upon us," seemed to thrill our souls. The deep voices of the older men sounded like a mighty organ, and the responses by the youthful choir made us feel that we were listening to the harmonies of heaven. Standing somewhat apart from the throng of devout worshippers, some of us, indeed, I think all, were completely overcome by the matchless sublimity of the music; the effect was somewhat exhausting—it raised one to the highest pitch of enjoyable excitement.

"Come," said the Matron at the conclusion of the service, "let us go and rest for we cannot endure more, even though it should be enjoyment." But, instead, we wandered about the vast cathedral, loth to leave until we had seen a few of the marvellous decorations. The quantities of porphyry, marble, jaspar rhodonite, malachite, and lapis-lazuli in floors, walls, and pillars bewildered us. The gold doors of the Ikonastas at the back of the altar, shutting off the inner sanctuary, where women are never admitted, are covered with paintings and mosaics of great value.

At the Centennial Exhibition I well remember being fascinated with the Russian exhibit, and bought for quite a sum a four-by-six inch slab of malachite; the man in charge casually remarked: "That is like the pillars in St. Isaac's, Miss." To my mind the pillars might have been a foot or two high, and then I thought how fine they must look, but on seeing four at either side of the altar some thirty feet high and the same number of lapis-lazuli, I felt that without visiting Russia one can have no realization of the accumulated treasure of the country. In England a friend said to one of the party, "Did you see any of this in Russia?" showing a scarf pin set with a piece of lapis-lazuli the size of a pea, perfect in color and highly valued by the owner. "Yes," was the crushing reply, "in one room at the summer palace of Tsarskoe Selo there are a dozen tables and a score of other articles made from the same precious stone." Not that it is inexpensive even in Russia, but the lavish expenditure of the Tsars from the time of Peter the Great has secured a wealth of rarest treasures. The railing about the chancel is of solid silver. The Ikons interested us very much, the first we had ever seen. They are sacred pictures worshipped by the people,—representations of Christ, the Madonna and Child, and of various saints, the especial favorite being St. Alexander Nevski, whose memory is held in great reverence by the Russians. The Ikons are usually about two feet square, covered with glass and framed elaborately; most of them are placed on inclined supports, and have exquisite lamps of gold, silver, or enamel hanging before them always lighted. With the exception of hands, face, and feet all the painting is covered with ornamental gold and silver plates. On many Ikons diamonds, sapphires, and other precious stones are set in the greatest profusion in the crowns, around the throats, and about the hands, making the effect dazzling and the value enormous; others have imitation stones of great brilliancy.

The first act of a Russian upon entering a church is to purchase a small candle which has previously been blessed. This he lights and places in one of the numerous small holders on the top of a massive silver or rare enamel candlestick, one of which stands in front of each Ikon. A large gayly decorated candle burns in the centre, surrounded by holders for one or two dozen smaller ones, which are nearly always filled by devotees. Then the worshipper goes to the framed picture, kisses the glass covering it, crosses himself, and continues his devotions. This continual kissing of Ikons is a fruitful source of diseases of the mouth among Russians, for the glasses being seldom cleaned a kind of thin crust is formed, which of course transmits any impurities of the skin. The sale of candles is a source of considerable revenue, a stall filled with all sizes being kept inside the door of each church. If a worshipper is very devout he will purchase a fine candle for twenty or thirty kopecks, but if very poor and not so religious he can do his duty for a tenth of the sum. After burning to a certain length the candles are removed by one of the numerous uniformed servants of the church; they are then melted down, made into new ones and sold over again. Is not this a very thrifty custom?

Intent upon their worship, the Russians pay no heed to sight-seers. They are superstitious to an incredible degree and in small matters carry it to an absurd extent. For example, when a man yawns, he crosses himself to prevent the devil from jumping down his throat. During service they have no especial time for crossing themselves, but whenever the inclination seizes them they cross with the thumb first and middle finger, signifying the Trinity; this is repeated three times, then prostrating themselves they touch the floor with their heads the same number of times and murmur in Russian: "God have mercy upon us."

The service of the Russo-Greek Church is by far the most imposing of any I have ever seen. During the prayer for the Tsar, when the doors of the Ikonastas are closed, the deep chanting of the choir, with the glorious voice of the officiating deacon intoning the prayer, impresses one with the solemnity of the occasion and the devotion of the people. No seats being allowed, strangers can wander about at will and seem to cause no commotion. To St. Isaac's we returned several times. The music and entire service on Sunday morning were very impressive, and we were content to stand until its close, although over two hours long. It is always better to stand where one cannot see the singers, as their appearance is unprepossessing; their long surplices reach the floor and are tied in at the waist; their heavy faces and unkempt hair detract from the feeling of devotion the music inspires. With one exception, the choir of St. Isaac's is the finest in Russia, its superior being the private choir of the Tsar which we could not hear. The squalor, poverty, and filth of a majority of the worshippers presented a terrible contrast to the magnificence of the churches, of which it is hopeless to attempt to give the slightest conception. St. Isaac's is worth over fifteen millions of dollars.

I was the only one of our party to ascend the great dome, and truly it was a hard climb. A half hour's steady walking up winding stairs and, finally, narrow iron ladders, brought me to the very top, but it was worth far more trouble and fatigue to see the wonderful view of the vast city from that height. The area covered by St. Petersburg seems to be illimitable; the buildings are close together, very large, but not high. Some writer speaks of three palaces side by side, so huge that to pass them requires a walk of half an hour, certainly every thing in Russia is on the same gigantic scale. From St. Isaac's dome one is able to realize more fully the daring of Peter in building his capital on that particular locality. It seemed to me that the quaking morass on which the city stands might some day swallow it all up. Scattered here and there are tall towers, where continual watch is kept for fire and the rising of the Neva. The story of the building is so well known that it is needless to enter into details, but the perishing of one hundred thousand workmen from the cold, wet, and poisonous marsh gas is a sad side to its history. Peter's expressed desire to have his city "a window looking out into Europe" was fully realized.

After the first evening spent in this wonderful cathedral, wearied with the impressive service and satiated with magnificence, we drove for nearly the entire length of the Nevski Prospect, the longest and finest street in St. Petersburg, and then to the railway station to say adieu to our Squire, who left for America *via* Moscow and Bremen. It was a sad moment when the first break was made in our party, and with genuine regret we said good-by to one who had proved himself an excellent companion, and whose untiring kindness added much to the pleasure of our trip.

"What shrine is that, Pilly?" asked the Matron, as we passed a small open temple returning from the station. "Law, ma'am," said Pilly, "that's no shrine, it's only a little pray-God place." All over the city are these "little pray-God places" where the devout people enter, cross themselves, drink some holy water, leave an offering of a few kopecks, and go on their way. The numerous shrines have been erected to saints, or in remembrance of some holy deed, or as thank-offerings. Some twenty years since a man shot at the late Emperor as he passed through the gate of the summer garden. On that spot has been erected one of St. Petersburg's most elaborate shrines, as a token of gratitude that his Majesty's life was spared. A fine cathedral is now being erected where the dynamite explosion occurred which so cruelly ended the life of the " Tsar Liberator," as he is called.

At many churches unleavened bread in small loaves was offered for sale. It was strange to see people drinking holy water, instead of merely using it for crossing; the cups are rarely cleansed, and it cannot be a healthful practice to drink the water where so many grimy hands have been dipped, but the superstitious people probably think drinking the blessed water is more efficacious than a slight outward application. But, oh! they are so filthy! Is it not said that the Russian moujik, clad in sheepskin, is thoroughly bathed but three times, at birth, marriage, and death?

In passing shrines and cathedrals the men remove their hats and cross themselves devoutly, and during our first drives it was quite startling to see our coachman suddenly remove his head-gear, fling back his shock of hair, and cross himself, while the horses went on their own way, evidently accustomed to the devotion of their drivers. In most of the shops Ikons are placed in a conspicuous position, with lighted lamps hanging before them. Strangers are expected to pay some reverence; while standing before them a man must remove his hat or meet with a reproof, for outwardly the Russians are undeniably devout. In every cathedral is a shrine containing the emblematical tomb of our Lord; this consists of a large silver or gold ornamented casket with a glass top, painted on the under-side with a life-size figure of Christ. They are, of course, considered very holy, and on Easter and Christmas eve the top with the painted figure is carried into the centre of the church and there worshipped and kissed by thousands of people. The incense swung by the archbishop has a pungent and delicious odor. After the service, the officiating priest takes a small cross down among the people, who scramble and push to get an opportunity to kiss it. We saw some forlorn babies baptized after the Sunday-morning service, and it was quite harrowing to see the rough way they were held by an assistant while with a spoon the priest forced some of the noxious holy water down their throats. When in England Peter the Great was much pleased with the tall old-fashioned clocks and ordered one placed in each church in St. Peterburg, where they still remain in droll contrast to the splendor of their surroundings.

CHAPTER V.

MORE CHURCHES, SHRINES, AND MONASTERIES—DRIVES ABOUT THE CAPITAL.

WHY do not more people go to Russia? That question kept recurring to my mind all through those pleasant days spent in the wonderful country. Why do tourists so continually choose the beaten tracks of travel, content often to spend much time in London and Paris shops? Not that shops are to be despised,— far be it from me to suggest that, —but there are so many countries of such absorbing interest and the beauties of which are unknown to most of us, that the taste for travel and adventure is not at all difficult to acquire. My ideas concerning

Russia were vague. I thought of a vast country in which there might be much of interest, but had formed no idea of the stupendous amount of sight-seeing one could enjoy in St. Petersburg and Moscow. While we accomplished a great deal, I feel a strong desire to return and settle down for three or four months in order to go about leisurely and see more of the social life, which can only be enjoyed in the winter.

After a good night's rest, we were ready to begin our adventures early the following morning after our arrival. The weather was superb and we were impatient to be off. Pilly systematized our arrangements, and we found no fatigue in carrying them out. A smart landau with a pair of excellent black horses held a happy party, and off we started down the Nevski, which is a broad, clean avenue, three miles long. Churches and shrines innumerable we wished to visit, but were forced to content ourselves with a few of the finest. The Kazan cathedral, on the Nevski, is a large, imposing building, a copy of St. Peter's at Rome, with which it compares rather unfavorably. The interior is gorgeous with monoliths of Finnish granite, Ikons, and candlesticks of great beauty. The Ikonastas or screen and balustrade, are made of solid silver, which was an offering from the "zealous don Cossacks" after Napoleon's retreat from Moscow. In the centre of the screen is a design in precious stones.

To this cathedral belongs the celebrated Ikon, called "Our Lady of Kazan," one of the most valuable in Russia. It is set with myriads of precious stones of the finest quality; one huge sapphire, worth many thousand pounds, was an offering from a well-known grand duchess. Just below this stone was formerly a perfect diamond of great size. A story was told us of a princess who, while at her devotions, feeling the pangs of hunger, bit out the fine stone, hiding it under her tongue. The theft being discovered, the clever Russian police soon found the culprit, and, after her tongue was torn out, she was exiled to Siberia. Moral: Always go to service after a satisfying meal. In this same church are many flags captured in battle from Turkey, Persia, and France, and also huge keys of captured fortresses, which looked as if they might have belonged to a giant's castle.

Driving past the Admiralty Square, we saw the famous equestrian statue of Peter, which is striking in its graceful and spirited pose; the charger is crushing under his foot the serpent, emblematical of the difficulties encountered and surmounted by the

Great Tsar. Of other fine statues there are scores. Nicholas I. on horseback, Catherine II., and several others of emperors, generals, and a fine statue in the well kept summer-gardens to Kyrlof, the great Russian satirist and translator of La Fontaine's fables. The work on the figure is excellent, and the pedestal well worth careful examination. On the four sides are representations of different fables, and the delicate carving and tracery are done with the utmost care.

Across one of the numerous bridges spanning the Neva we drove to the fortress, in which stands the celebrated cathedral of St. Peter and St. Paul. The cathedral is of fine proportions, and the tall, slender spire, being heavily gilded, is dazzling to one's eyes. Nearly all the sovereigns of Russia, with their families, are buried here. According to the rules of the Russian Church, the marble tombs are of the simplest description, those of the Tsars and Tsaritas being distinguished by the Russian eagle, in gold, on each of the four corners. The tomb of the martyred Tsar, Alexander II., is especially guarded; the beautiful flowers with which it is covered are renewed daily in large cases, and all about the space allotted to the last resting-place of the late Tsar are scores of wreaths of laurel, silver and gold, sent by patriotic societies and communities as tokens of loyal sympathy and regret for his terrible fate, which to us seems so undeserved and so cruel. I entreated, and Pilly offered a bribe for a flower or two from a fresh wreath sent by the Emperor the previous day, but, true to his orders, the guard positively refused to allow it to be touched. Unfortunate monarch! his terrible end was a base requital for his emancipation act, by which myriads of serfs were liberated. It gave us a thrill to stand beside the tomb of Peter the Great, that remarkable man who created the Russia of the present day, and to whose insatiable ambition most of the glory of the wonderful country is due.

Within this very fortress where the cathedral stands, Peter imprisoned his son Alexis and his unfortunate wife for treason, and, from the effect of tortures inflicted, the wretched man died. While I feel a strong inclination to devote much space to the life and career of Peter, more has been written of him than any other character of Russian history, and so well written that it would be presumption in me to do more than casually allude to him. The small cottage where he lived while superintending the building of that vast city stands near the cathedral of Peter and Paul. A building has been erected which entirely covers the cottage, to protect it from decay. One room, consecrated as a chapel, contains the most holy Ikon in St. Petersburg; it is of great age, and the Russians believe it to have been painted by St. Luke; the colors are very dark, and the face of Christ is haggard, showing traces of great suffering. It accompanied Peter in all his campaigns, and was held before the soldiers to increase their enthusiasm, and they carried it at " Poltava," which proved so disastrous a battle to Charles XII. and his forces. It is often sent to the bedside of sick people, accompanied by a priest, who prays to it for the afflicted one; the price for visiting may be one or two hundred rubles, according to the circumstances of people sending for it. In the room adjoining the chapel are numerous articles made by Peter's skilful hands: a large table, carved chair, stool, and candlesticks, also the boat he built and sailed.

Proofs of the ignorance and superstition of the people are seen in the large cases full of miniature arms, legs, heads, and even whole bodies, sent by sick people to be prayed for, and representing the part of the body afflicted; offerings to the holy picture accompanied the bits of silver bodies, consisting of lockets, rings, brooches, and coins innumerable. Service was being held while we were in the cottage, and two women were weeping bitterly; evidently the prayers were being chanted for some dear one seriously ill,—perchance dying.

The military cathedral of Preobrajenski is large and imposing, and we were much interested in the fence surrounding it composed of cannon and chains taken from the Turks;

within are many flags captured in battle. The pillars give one the impression of palm-trees, a lance forming each leaf. In a glass case beside the altar lies a fine sword with rusty scabbard; it is the one worn by Alexander II. when assassinated, and alas! the rust is caused by his blood. Near the case are uniforms belonging to him and his two predecessors. We drove to the American and English Embassies on the Palace quay, passed the Winter Palace and the homes of some of the Grand Dukes; it is quite the most fashionable drive in winter, and must be beautiful with the frozen Neva on the one hand and magnificent architecture on the other.

The bridges in St. Petersburg are especially worthy of notice, the "Nicholas" being one of the finest I have ever seen; it is broad and beautifully constructed. The town being intersected by arms of the Neva, there is need of numerous bridges. The crowd on the Nevski is cosmopolitan; one can always see Russians, Turks, Armenians, Jews, Poles, Greeks, and of course Americans. The few Russian women we saw attracted us very much. The street-car service is excellent in St. Petersburg, but drosky driving was so expeditious and cheap, that we did not use the trams; besides, the people looked better at a distance than when we were crowded in a car. The shops are numerous and excellent, and filled with most attractive goods; the work of the jewellers is fine, and we saw much and bought a little of the famous enamel, which is as beautiful as it is expensive. Russian leather is a misnomer; we tried unsuccessfully to find some in many shops, but at last Pilly enlightened us by saying: "Bless your heart, miss, there aint any Russia leather nearer than Austria."

The lace and embroidery we found reasonable and very effective, but oh! the bronzes;—those of my readers who visited the Centennial will remember the gorgeous display of bronzes, the designs are so fine and the work beautifully done. The great bazaar facing the Nevski, where ten thousand merchants are said to be engaged in business, looks as if it belonged to some Eastern city; men of different nationalities are busy there, and, although small, the shops are filled with goods of every description.

A drive across the Neva to the famous islands outside the city gave us a little rest after the exhausting day. At sunset we were standing on the point of "Kammenoi-Ostrof" or "Stone Island," where many wealthy St. Petersburg families have their summer homes. The view was lovely and the clouds brilliant, and, wandering about the islands, we enjoyed the tranquillity of the place. There are few Russians who are without country homes, and in all the villages and towns within a radius of fifty or more miles, there are picturesque residences belonging to all classes,— nobility, gentry and tradespeople; but few of the houses can compare with the villas at Newport, Lenox, and Bar Harbor.

The monastery of Alexander Nevski is one of the most celebrated in Russia. It stands at the extremity of the Nevski Prospect and occupies a large space; there are seven churches within the grounds, and the cathedral built by Catherine II. is one of the largest in St. Petersburg. (The monastery was founded by Peter in honor of the canonized Grand Duke, whose name it bears, and who vanquished the Swedes and Teutonic knights in the thirteenth century.)

It is very finely decorated with marbles and precious stones; the magnificent altar-piece is by Raphael Mengs, and there are excellent copies of Guido, Rubens, and Perugino. The shrine of Alexander Nevski is of massive silver, containing nearly four thousand pounds of pure metal, and magnificently wrought in various designs. In consecrated grounds about the monastery are buried many members of the wealthy Russian families, and large sums are paid for the privilege of burying the dead in such a holy place. The graves are very close together as the space is somewhat limited, and we saw many fresh flowers marking those graves most recently made. The crypt of the Cathedral of the Annunciation contains tombs of several of the most illustrious families in Russia; they are very ornate, and the rarest marbles are used for the floors and walls.

The place is so tranquil that the thought of death loses much of its terror. In striking contrast to these elaborate tombs, is the simple bronze tablet marking the last resting-place of the great General Suvaroff, who made the tablet with his own hands, inscribing it simply " Here lies Suvaroff." The singing by the monks of this monastery is celebrated, and we enjoyed the music intensely; the singers have long, fair, crinkled hair, and their voices are wonderful. I never can forget the music we were privileged to hear in both St. Petersburg and Moscow; it almost made us forget the cares aud sorrows of life, and lifted our souls into a state of ecstatic enjoyment.

"Now you 've heard the monks sing—don't you want to hear the nuns?" said our thoughtful guide, and of course we did. The drive to the convent was a long one, and after we left the Nevski the pavements were rough and in rather bad condition, but we saw much of the oldest part of the city and were on the direct road to Moscow. Just beyond our destination stands the Moscow gate, from which the post-road starts for the old capital, four hundred miles away. We found the convent large, scrupulously clean, and very attractive. The singing was charming and the female voices harmonized well, but after hearing such fine singing by the male choirs we missed the deep bass tones which had so thrilled us. The Mother Superior was very gracious to us, thanks to Pilly, who evidently knew her, and who skilfully slipped a small offering into her hand while bowing profoundly. Certainly, he was remarkably clever in the way he took us to see the best of every thing, and his tips were much smaller than we would have dared to offer the lordly creatures who showed us about palaces and museums. Although Russia is distinctly a country of fees, through our guide's judicious management we found a very moderate sum covered all expenditure in that direction. We had anticipated much trouble in going about the city and fancied that sight-seeing would be attended with many unpleasant red-tape details. I had visions of being followed by stern officials, stopped for explanations as to my purpose in visiting the country, and eavesdropping on all sides, but, on the contrary, no place could possibly be pleasanter to go about in, and everywhere we met the greatest kindness and courtesy. One regret was ever in my mind, that we could not remain months instead of weeks in Russia.

The hotel chambermaid evidently considered water very harmful, whether applied outwardly or internally, and a cold tub every morning filled her soul with horror, but finding I was firm, she overcame her scruples with the aid of a ruble or two. In most of the shops French is spoken; but once or twice the Matron and Madame endeavored to shop unaided by Pilly, with disastrous results to themselves. A very little Russian is of great assistance, and a few every-day phrases should be learned before visiting the country, for one feels so helpless hearing people speak in a language which is absolutely unlike any thing in Europe, Asia, or Africa, unless it might be a combination of *all*.

The droskies in Petersburg have one peculiarity lacking in those in Moscow. As can be seen, they are very narrow and without sides or back; add to this the most rapid, reckless driving, and it is very easy to understand why the necessity arises for a man to hold fast the woman with whom he is driving. It looked very strange to us to see what might be called a still waltz going on in every drosky, but being the custom of the country, it lost its strangeness, and we soon became accustomed to it.

The broad avenues of St. Petersburg must present a brilliant appearance in winter, being crowded with sledges and *troïkas* driven rapidly and noiselessly over the snow. The driving is so reckless that there is an average of one person killed daily, but, fortunately, the law is not the same as in France, where any one run over is fined for obstructing the thoroughfare, and I suppose the fine is proportionate to the injury received.

H. I. M. THE EMPEROR OF RUSSIA.

CHAPTER VI.

DAYS AT TSARSKOE SELO AND PETERHOF.

WE spent a very enjoyable day at Tsarskoe Selo, the favorite summer residence of the late Tsar, but where the present imperial family never resides. The town from which the palace takes its name is situated twenty-two versts from St. Petersburg. A drive of ten minutes from the railway station, during which we passed a mammoth orangery, of course, belonging to the imperial estate, brought us to the enormous and imposing palace. At the main entrance, which faces a large court, there were a number of lackeys standing to receive us. They wore the imperial livery of gray, trimmed with narrow bands of gilt and elaborately stamped in black, with the double-headed eagle of Russia. It would be an interesting matter to know how many servants are employed in the different palaces, as there are always so many standing about. Pilly told us that in the royal stables livery is provided for two thousand men, and at Tsarskoe Selo, where the grounds are very extensive and kept in perfect condition, there are six hundred gardeners working.

At the entrance of each palace and governmental offices stands a major-domo whose appearance is very imposing, wearing a scarlet coat reaching the ground, with five small capes edged with the elaborate bands to which reference has already been made, a startling hat, and carrying a long wand of office. All these men knew Pilly, who is evidently a prime favorite, and great liberty is accorded him. The Royal Chapel, where we were taken first, is said to be the most ornate in Russia, and we accepted the statement without doubting its truth, for, although small, it is perfectly gorgeous,—no other word will express it. Decorated in bright blue and gold, with paintings of the intensely high coloring so much affected by many Russian artists, in any other place it would seem distinctly vulgar, but there the effect is not unpleasing. The massive gold doors of the Ikonastas are especially fine, and above is a striking decoration in gold.

The balcony at the rear of the chapel was the favorite place of the late Tsar during service, and, standing where he had so often been, we tried to imagine his feelings, but without success. Although it may reasonably be supposed that his trials were no less than those of the rest of mankind, it is fairly certain that the good and evil within him strove for the victory, as in mortals of commoner clay. At all events, the existence of a Russian Emperor cannot be an enviable one in these troublous times. A friend told us that the present Empress lives in constant fear of some deed of violence being done to her husband; but for that terrible anxiety their lives might be so happy, for they, of all people, have in such profusion every luxury and pleasure this world can give.

The state apartments at Tsarskoe Selo are, of course, magnificent beyond description; the famous amber room, worth I dare not say how many millions of rubles, is marvellous. The walls of this very large apartment are covered nearly to the ceiling with small pieces perfectly fitted, making a smooth surface of opaque amber;

tables are inlaid with it, chandeliers ornamented with it, and all kinds of ornaments are carved from it; in glass cases are small articles cut from the clearest specimen that I ever saw. A chess-board, with elaborately carved men, is of the most exquisite workmanship, and bears the closest examination. The furniture is covered with brocade of the same color. All the amber was presented by Frederick the Great to Catherine II., that bold, ambitious, profligate woman, whose husband, Peter III., was strangled, probably by her order. However, with all her wickedness, cruel despotism, and reckless extravagance, Catherine did much to advance civilization in Russia.

The lapis-lazuli room, containing tables, candelabra, vases, and numerous other articles of the same rare mineral, has a floor of ebony, inlaid with mother-of-pearl, making a splendid effect. The bedrooms are hung with richest silks of different colors, one in rose-pink being perfectly exquisite. The bedroom of the Empress Catherine is decorated in an unusual way, having walls of porcelain and pillars of amethyst glass. The large Chinese room, connected with the private apartments of the late Empress, is fitted up in superb style; every thing was brought direct from China, the walls being made in sections for this especial room. The embroidered silk-hangings and furniture coverings are of the richest possible description; beautiful vases, genuine lacquer-ware, brilliant embroideries, and ornaments of all kinds are in reckless profusion. This wonderful room was formerly used for tea-drinkings, and is kept exactly as it was during the life of the late Empress. A number of inlaid tables holding rare china tea-sets are placed about the room, and every thing seems in readiness for guests to arrive and refresh themselves with "yellow tea," and oh, how we longed for a cup! The royal playroom is most unique, and fitted up as a gymnasium; how my heart stirred at the sight of a small mahogany toboggan slide, polished to the highest degree of smoothness; we were very hilarious when, sliding down on a square of red cloth, which takes one rapidly across the large room, and our enthusiasm won a smile from the serious lackey in attendance upon us.

The palace contains hundreds of rooms, of which we saw a large number; they are all crammed with bric-a-brac of every sort, malachite tables, huge candelabra, vases, writing-sets, and clocks, all set in gold bronze. We examined rare porcelain, pictures and ornaments of all kinds until our brains and eyes were weary, and we longed for a pine table. The inlaid floors in all the palaces were the finest we had ever seen, and the massive doors were of gold, silver, buhl, bronze, and rarest woods, heavily carved. It seemed strange that so little attention is paid to the comfort of bedrooms;—where and how they sleep seems to be the last problem the Russians consider. As for the innumerable servants, in palaces and houses of the nobility, they sleep on sofas, or the floor, just as it happens; there are as many as one hundred and fifty employed in one residence, each having a special duty, and always refusing to do any thing outside of that particular department.

The private apartments of Alexander I., kept exactly as he left them, are of great interest. His simple bedroom contains a camp bedstead; on a table are brushes, combs, shaving articles, and a pocket-handkerchief. In the room are his uniform, cap, and boots; the latter, being very long and narrow, are patched in several places. I have a confused recollection of banqueting- and ball-rooms, having walls covered with gold and silver and filled with mirrors and a superb collection of rare vases. The large grounds, some seventeen or eighteen miles in circumference, are laid out in the most elaborate manner, with pavilions, towers, Chinese village, artificial ruins, columns, statues, and many other strange devices. On the lake is kept a collection of boats of every description.

During our stay in Petersburg the annual fête at Peterhof was held in honor of her Majesty's birthday. All business was suspended in the capital, every one taking a holiday. Unfortunately it started to rain late in the afternoon, making it impossible to have the illuminations at Peterhof until the following evening (Sunday). The temptation to go and enjoy what we were certain would be a great spectacle proved too much for the Signorina and myself, so we started by the steamer at four o'clock, guarded by our faithful Pilly. The charming sail occupied about an hour, and arriving at Peterhof, Pilly hastened to secure one of the few good carriages at the wharf, but at an enormous rate, as on fête days Russian coachmen ask as much as they please, and generally get it too.

What an amount of sight-seeing we accomplished that afternoon! Pilly certainly proved himself a model guide, never wasting a moment, and always taking us to the most desirable places. First of all to the beautiful palace, where, on account of the holiday, no one was

Tsarskoe Selo and Peterhof. 111

admitted without a special permit, which, however, had been secured by our thoughtful courier. The Emperor does not live there, but has a magnificent summer residence some two miles distant, and where strangers are not allowed to go. The State Palace stands on a high terrace, below which the fountains and innumerable devices for water extend some hundreds of yards. As we drove through the long park before reaching the palace, we saw some of the elaborate preparations made for the illuminations. Large frames of odd, artistic designs, covered with small colored glasses, each holding a candle, were on either side of the road. By the way, our expectations as to the beauty of the display were naturally high, as we had been told that the Tsar had given one hundred and twenty thousand rubles, or sixty thousand dollars, for one evening's illumination. We were charmed with the palace; in striking contrast with many others it seemed very home-like, and excellent taste was displayed throughout. At the entrance, with a dozen or more lackeys, stood one of the Tsar's eight Nubian footmen; being very tall and very black, dressed in Eastern costume, he was an imposing figure. The halls and staircases were beautifully decorated with ferns, palms, and other plants. The suite of rooms occupied by the Kaiser during his late visit were very cheerfully and exquisitely fitted up. Trying the couches and chairs, we found them most luxurious, all being stuffed with eider-down. Room after room we passed through, all containing beautiful articles of the rarest description. The dressing-room has the most exquisite mirrors, and toilet arrangements of Dresden china, which looked much too delicate and fragile for a man's use. Among the most attractive of the hundreds of rooms, the White Banquet-Hall stands pre-eminent. Large, with marble walls, white enamelled furniture, upholstered in white brocade velvet, with hangings of the same, marble tables scattered about, the only color being in the chandeliers, which are of amethyst crystal, the effect of the room is dazzlingly beautiful. One highly interesting apartment contains a collection of over eight hundred female portraits, painted by order of Catherine II., by Rotari, who made a journey through Russia for the purpose of finding different models. They are all beautiful girls in picturesque national costumes, and one is impressed with the inventive genius of the artist who was able to give a different expression to so many faces.

The ornamental water-works are of the most elaborate description. The garden is laid out in terraces adorned with devices of every kind; they are considered to be but little inferior to those at Versailles. The cascades are beautiful in the daytime, but at night, when illuminated with colored lights from underneath, it was like fairy-land. The English Palace, so-called on account of the gardens which belong to it having been laid out by a landscape gardener brought from England for the purpose, is a square, unpretentious building, now used for drilling boys for the royal choir. In one room there is a spirited portrait of Catherine the Great on horseback, in male attire, at the head of her army, and also one of Elizabeth, attended by a negro runner.

A French villa a mile distant from the park, stands in the midst of a fine garden, where the flowers were growing luxuriously. At the back of the villa the grounds are elaborately laid out, and although small the plan is charming. The house is furnished *à la Louis Seize*, the brocade hangings being of delicate and appropriate colors, the doors are inlaid with Sevres china, and there is much to admire in the ornamentation of the house. Every thing is in order, should their Majesties choose to step in and stay for a day or two,— even the delicate china is in readiness, and being designed for this villa is of course in keeping with the prevailing style.

The model cottage within the park limits is a small two-story picturesque building, a fac-simile of what a peasant's home should be, but from the reports of the abject poverty of many Russian subjects, it is probably only an ideal home. The simple wooden furniture is of artistic design; the blue and white china and plain glass are thoroughly appropriate, and ready for use.

In several of the rooms are displayed many bread-trenchers and salt-boxes of carved wood, presented to different Tsars when visiting small towns and villages in the empire. The Russian custom is to offer a freshly baked loaf of bread on the trencher, the small box filled with salt being laid on top of the loaf,—a very hospitable and attractive welcome it seems to me. The straw cottage, a favorite resort of Catherine II., is a most deceptive building. The exterior is small, and before going in we supposed the rooms would be tiny, but to our surprise the entrance hall seemed enormous, and we found it was due to the ceiling and walls being lined with mirrors. The artificial vines

Tsarskoe Selo and Peterhof. 117

trained over the walls successfully simulate real foliage. Catherine, accompanied by a few favorites, went often to this charming cottage for tea on summer afternoons, all court formalities being laid aside. We heard much about this Empress' extravagance; there seemed to be no limit to her goodness to favorites, but to those unfortunate enough to incur her displeasure, she spared no torture. Prince Potemkin, for a long time her lover, had unbounded influence over this bad but brilliant woman, and the amount of money she squandered upon him was perfectly fabulous.

We were charmed with the small mill where Nicholas and his children often went and played at humble life, although not with such an extreme affectation of simplicity as Marie Antoinette and her court at Trianon. A Pompeian villa we of course enjoyed seeing every detail being correct. On a high elevation stands the beautiful Belvedere. It is built in the Greek style, of gray granite with Ionic columns of white marble. One has from this pavilion an extensive view of the surrounding country, which is somewhat picturesque. Some very fine statuary stands at the entrance. There is a comfortable elevator inside, but only for royal use. The rooms are well appointed, the furniture and china being especially designed for the building.

Two small islands in the lake, the Empress and the Olga, are reached in an unique manner. A square, wooden platform, holding four chairs, is pulled to and fro by ropes passing through rings on the top of iron posts, one being at each corner of the platform. They are worked by two men-of-war's men in the Russian naval uniform. We enjoyed this novel experience, and after reaching the Empress isle, we found the so-called summer-house a picturesque villa, perfect in all its appointments; the china, decorated with sea-weed, and with handles and feet of coral, was in keeping with the island. Flowers were plentiful, and we picked some of the largest pansies I have ever seen; a thriving tree is growing from an acorn taken from George Washington's grounds, and presented to Nicholas I. by a brother of Charles Sumner. Near by is the cottage of Peter the Great—a square, unpretentious building, containing much of his clothing and furniture.

We were not allowed to enter Montplaisir, a low Dutch summer-house, as preparations were being made for the royal party to drink tea there after driving about to see the illuminations. By eight o'clock it was growing dark, and needing some rest after so much sight-seeing, we ventured to partake of a Russian dinner before going out to see the grand display. We were told that the lighting of the various devices required eighteen hundred men working steadily for more than half an hour.

After dinner we started to walk through the park; the crowd was great, and a multitude of peasants in national costumes made a pictuesque effect; there was perfect order among the tens of thousands of expectant people. To give any adequate idea of the grandeur of the display would require pages of high-flown language with adjectives *ad nauseam*. It was one's idea of fairy-land, and now the evening seems like an entrancing dream. Standing on the terrace in front of the palace, we looked down upon fountains, cascades, and artificial streams all lighted from below with various colors. At the end of this long avenue of water was an enormous sun with the imperial cipher in the centre; probably this design was made of tin, but illuminated with the strongest electric light it resembled a mass of diamonds; the effect of this shining on the water was dazzling. On each side of the broad walk were frames of various shapes, stars, crescents, crosses, and geometrical designs, all blazing with colored lights. In the great fountain Sampson, so called from a large bronze figure tearing open the jaws of a lion, from which rushes a stream eighty feet high, the color of the water was constantly changing, making a grand effect. Marly, Peter's cottage, seen across the miniature illuminated lake, looked as if built of the palest yellow alabaster; the way in which this plain little house was lighted seemed to transform it into a fairy palace. Why continue the details of the wonderful *ensemble;* the scene could not be surpassed in beauty, and we walked about as in a dream. In some places the effects were so exquisite, that I could only look stupidly before me and pinch myself to find out whether I was really in the flesh or transported to the realm of fancy. We were in a state of expectancy, knowing that the Emperor and Empress were driving through the park, and we waited to see them near the middle of the long avenue where the Tsar's Circassian body-guard was stationed. Few precautions for the safety of the royal party were taken, except that the way was kept clear by this singularly handsome corps of soldiers dressed in their national uniform. The thousands of people lining both sides of the avenue waited patiently for a sight of their majesties, and after a few moments of expectation we heard cheer after cheer from the direction in which they were coming. We had an excellent position near the road and could see very well.

Soon two big English breaks came in sight, followed by several smaller traps. In the first were the Emperor, Empress, their children, and near relatives; the second was occupied by friends, and the carriages by ladies and gentlemen of the court. The breaks were each drawn by eight horses with postilions and outriders in scarlet and gold. The crowd displayed great enthusiasm and we were delighted to have seen the imperial party. We looked at the approach to Montplaisir, which of course was beautifully lighted and decorated, making a brilliant effect through the trees. The music by several military bands stationed through the park was excellent, and some stirring airs from Glinka's "Life for the Tsar," were enthusiastically appreciated by the dense throng of people. All through the park the display was elaborate, and after walking miles and seeing much that was novel, we left for the railway station at eleven P.M., when the fireworks were commencing. We had abundant opportunity to rest and talk over the pleasures of the excursion; as the train being delayed we did not reach our hotel until two o'clock on Monday morning, so we did not desecrate Sunday by returning on that day. How fine it all was! We considered ourselves lucky in having seen the display, and in a feeble way we began to realize how great the power of the Tsar is. Every thing belongs to him, and from infancy the heir-apparent is taught that he is the sole ruler of the empire, and to his will all must bow;

he is reverenced by the masses as a God, and there is no possibility of giving an adequate idea of his riches of palaces and villas; he has at least half a hundred, all filled with the most rare and expensive articles.

CHAPTER VII.

A GLIMPSE OF THE HERMITAGE.

How shall I be able to do even slight justice to the Hermitage, that wonderful museum, conceded by antiquarians and scholars to contain the richest treasures ever accumulated in one place. Founded by Catherine II. in a small pavilion attached to the Winter Palace, it was enlarged by her in order to furnish room for the vast collection of fine pictures which it contains. The Empress used the Hermitage as a refuge from the cares, responsibilities, and formalities of her position; her evenings were spent there, and she gathered about her artists, poets, men of letters, philosophers, wits, and musicians. Certain rules observed by the privileged fre-

THE EMPRESS OF RUSSIA.

quenters of the Hermitage are so apt, that I will insert them here:

"I. Leave your rank outside as well as your hat, and especially your sword.

"II. Leave your right of precedence, your pride, and any similar feeling out-side the door.

"III. Be gay, but do not spoil any thing; do not break or gnaw any thing.

"IV. Sit, stand, walk, as you will, without reference to anybody.

"V. Talk moderately, but not very loud, to make the ears and hearts of others ache.

"VI. Argue without anger and without excitement.

"VII. Neither sigh, nor yawn, nor make anybody heavy.

"VIII. In all innocent games whatever one proposes, let all join.

"IX. Eat whatever is sweet and savory, but drink moderately, so that each may find his legs on leaving the room.

"X. Tell no tales out of school; whatever goes in at one ear must go out of the other before leaving the room.

"A transgressor against these rules shall, on the testimony of two witnesses, for every offence drink a glass of cold water, not excepting the ladies, and further read a page of 'Telemachiade' aloud. Whoever breaks any three of these rules during the same evening shall commit six lines of the 'Telemachiade' to memory; and whoever offends against the tenth rule shall not be again admitted."

The building is very imposing, and for beauty and costliness scarcely equalled in Europe. It forms a great parallelogram 515 by 375 feet, with a magnificent entrance. The vestibule, is upheld by ten caryatides twelve or fifteen feet high, cut from granite, with statues of sculptors, artists, and painters, are placed in niches, and you enter a great hall supported by the usual colonnade of beautiful pillars cut from Finland granite. Now that we have passed the entrance, I hardly know where to begin. Those of my readers who have been privileged to visit this wonderful place will appreciate how difficult it will be to give an adequate idea of the vast collection of statuary, paintings, jewels, coins, and antiquities, which it contains. It seems to me that a knowledge of the contents of this vast museum would constitute a liberal education.

To the rooms filled with the Kertch collection we went first; it is said to be the most remarkable and unique in the world. Found in the Cimmerian Bosphorus, it proves the existence of Greek colonies six hundred years before the birth of Christ. A sarcophagus, made of cypress and yew, with skeleton probably deposited twenty-two hundred years ago, is in a remarkable state of preservation, and the vermilion coloring of some of the ornaments can still be traced. Cases line the walls and fill the rooms, containing rare coins, medals, jewels of every kind, and of such delicate workmanship that it seems as if they could not have been made by human hands. Among the Grecian curios is an old helmet, which still contains the head of the owner, the cracked skull and injured helmet indicating that a stone was thrown with tremendous force from a sling, which expeditiously ended the life of the warrior. The delicate tracery of the goldsmith's work surpasses in beauty any thing of the present day; and there is such a bewildering collection that one is at a loss where to begin looking. There are many terra-cotta toys found in children's tombs, household utensils, vases, lamps, iridescent glass, rare scarabei, and various ornaments for men and women. The most valuable case is in the room containing treasures of a priestess of Ceres. The trappings of her horses were buried with her, also sandals, exquisite *repousée* looking-glass of bronze, gilt bracelets, buttons, necklace, and diadem, all used by her. There is also an extensive collection of Scythian, Siberian, and Russian antiquities. In the numismatic collection of over 200,000 specimens are many coins of ancient Greece and Rome; three large cases are filled with old English coins, among them some belonging to the days before the Roman Conquest. Two gems, perhaps the finest and most important extant, are signed " Dexamenos," and their design is a heron flying.

It was a source of genuine regret

that we could not spend more time among these relics of by-gone days. When of such interest to us, what an absorbing delight they must be to the classical scholar. We lingered among those wonderful antiquities, until Pilly exclaimed in a tone of despair: "Ladies and gentleman and Miss, the Hermitage closes at three, and you have seen nothing yet." He took a keen delight in showing us special objects in each collection, and always selected the most interesting.

Now for the armory, filling, I think, eight or nine rooms. It is by far the finest collection in the world, and we were told that it would equal a combination of all similar displays in Europe. Its value is beyond computation. There is every kind of armor for man and horse, ancient and modern, heavy and light, ornate and simple, Persian, Indian, Japanese, Bokharian, Albanian, German, French, Tartar, Arabian, Polish, and Italian. A huge Scandinavian war-trumpet interested us. Having been so recently in "the land of the Viking," everything connected with that grand country, and especially with the days of so long ago, had a fascination for us. Of firearms there are every conceivable kind and from various countries,—poisonous daggers from the East, scimitars, Italian stilettos, and swords by the hundreds, some with scabbards entirely encrusted with diamonds and other precious stones, with the hilts a mass of glittering gems; room after room it was the same story.

Two sets of horse trappings, presented by the Sultan to Nicholas I., one after the treaty of Adrianople in 1829, and the other in 1833, are of royal magnificence. The first we could scarcely believe genuine velvet saddle-cloth studded with diamonds, bridle, pistol holsters, and gold stirrups all set with the same precious stones, but the second stupefied us. Saddle-cloth and bridle are a mass of brilliants of the purest water, while the brightness of those on the pistol holsters is perfectly dazzling, and it is worth a king's ransom.

When satiated with gems and the magnificent armor, we betook ourselves to the galleries, little realizing what a treat was in store for us. There are seventeen hundred paintings by the best masters of the Italian, Spanish, French, Dutch, Flemish, and German schools ; also it is said to be the only gallery on the Continent with a collection of English pictures. It is especially rich in Flemish and Spanish works, including many Murillos, Velasquez, Rubens, Van Dycks, Teniers, Vanderhelsts, Rembrandts, Wouvermans,

Paul Potters, etc. Raphael's frescos fill two rooms, and were purchased in 1861 with the Campana Museum in Rome. In each of the eight rooms, in addition to the pictures, are many magnificent vases, tables, and candelabra of rare Siberian minerals, many pieces of malachite, all of enormous size, set in gold bronze. The violet and ribbon jasper, we thought finest until we saw some large candelabra of rhodonite, a rare pink, variegated stone which is perfectly exquisite and cannot be purchased, being worked only in the royal manufactory for the use of the imperial family and given by them to friends, as are also several varieties of porphyry and jasper; these gorgeous ornaments alone are worth going miles to see, and these rare stones are to a great extent kept in Russia. It seemed to me that the workmen must have been possessed of great artistic talent, for the carving of them is done with consummate skill.

So many pictures charmed us that merely to mention the names would be wearisome to the reader, but I must speak of a few which impressed me most. In the Italian school "Perseus and Andromeda," by Tintoretto, is exquisite in coloring. "David with the Head of Goliath," by Guido Réni, is a strong, dark picture. "The Virgin at School," by the same master, is a group of fresh, innocent-looking children. Carlo Dolci's "Saint Cecilia" is very pleasing. The principal picture by Rubens is Mary Magdalene bathing the Saviour's feet. "The Expulsion of Hagar," also Rubens', is exquisite, but to me Vandervelde's treatment of the subject is finer, and is one of the most touchingly strong pictures in the Dresden gallery. In one of the rooms filled with Raphael's frescos is his famous "Virgin and Child," presented by Alexander II. to the late Empress on the twenty-fifth anniversary of their marriage. Leonardo da Vinci's "Holy Family" is a well-known work of great merit. Paul Potter's "Watch Dog" is perfect; the brilliant clear eye and matted coat are remarkably executed, and the nine pictures by him are of great interest. Wouverman's numerous works are worth careful examination. No. 1,017 is one of the very few pictures painted by him without the ubiquitous white horse.

An allegorical picture, "The Infant Hercules Strangling the Serpents," painted by Sir Joshua Reynolds by order of Catherine II., represents the difficulties which beset the empire and were overcome by it. The Empress was so pleased with this picture that she sent the artist a gold snuffbox and her portrait set in diamonds;

there are several other fine works of the great English painter. The collection of Rembrandts is of great interest, and as there are specimens of his work at all periods on many subjects, he can be studied here better than anywhere else. One of Peter denying Christ attracted special attention; the light on the picture was from a candle, and the deep shadows seemed weirdly impressive. Rubens' " Descent from the Cross " is a repetition of the famous one in Antwerp, and of great artistic beauty.

In a room devoted to game and fruit pictures is an exquisite marble "Cupid and Psyche," of Canova. How clearly one can see the master's hand in all his works; this exquisite piece is so natural that one would fain waken both figures with a kiss. In the French school Boucher, Watteau, Greuze, Nicholas Poussin, and Claude Lorraine are represented.

Canova's "Hebe" is also in this apartment.

A few words about the numerous Russian pictures and I am done. "Sunrise on the Black Sea," "The Deluge," and "The Creation of the World," all by the celebrated marine painter Aivazofski, are strange and quite unlike the work of any other artist. The latter is the most extraordinary, and the chaos from which the world is emerging is indescribably weird. His work is strong and daring, and always recognizable even to a casual observer. Neff's flesh painting is especially fine. The most striking picture in the collection is Brülow's "Last Days of Pompeii," and is considered the most important work of the Russian school. The deservedly famous "Venus" of the Hermitage, a well preserved Greek statue found at Rome, is one of the most exquisite pieces of antique statuary found in Europe, and we were touched by its beauty. We greatly enjoyed Canova's work, so exquisite in its details, and the drapery on his figures has a peculiarly diaphanous effect. A superb statue of Mephistopheles fills one's ideas of Satanic cunning. The position of the figure, the satirical expression, the tense muscles of fingers and toes, suggest extreme *diablerie*. Two fine pieces by Rauch—one of Voltaire, the other of Ivan the Terrible—are of great merit.

Our time was too limited to enable us to see the Library, with its rare engravings, manuscripts, and priceless missals. The collection of Greek and Etruscan vases is the most extensive in Europe, and the gallery of drawings contains twelve thousand works by eminent masters. The memory of Peter the Great is held in great reverence by the Russians; there are souvenirs of him everywhere, and we felt a strong inclination to see all we could of the articles made and used by him. His gallery in the Hermitage is crammed with interesting things; his strength must have been in proportion to his great stature, for the iron walking stick he carried we could barely raise an inch from the floor. We examined his books, mathematical instruments, lathe and carving tools. His effigy in a suit embroidered by his wife, Catherine I., is in the centre of the gallery. An interesting object to us was a cast made of his face when alive; the long hair and mustache are jet black. The horse he rode at Pultava, and several favorite dogs, stand in a glass case, but either the horse must have shrunken in the preserving process, or Peter must have had both feet on the ground when astride the fiery charger, as it is now not much taller than a Lower Canadian pony. He worked with many different materials; turning, carving, and embossing, he tried them all.

Just before we left the gallery, Pilly came toward us, saying in a mysterious whisper: "Come, follow me at once, don't speak, and try not to breathe more than is absolutely necessary." Naturally we nearly choked in a mad endeavor to cease inhaling oxygen, and were quickly taken to the private state apartments, which are closed to the general public. This magnificent suite of rooms has a fine view of the Neva, and at different times has been occupied by the Prince and Princess of Wales, the Shah of Persia, and the late Emperor Frederick, when Crown Prince, with his wife. We were singularly fortunate in seeing these rooms, which were in readiness for the Khedive's son, who was to arrive the following day. Fitted up with the greatest luxury, they are home-like and comfortable to the highest degree. Seeing the furniture uncovered, flowers placed all about the rooms, and even writing materials laid ready, Pilly said "Ladies, you are very lucky; I know every part of this place well, but I never saw these rooms when in order for royal guests, and in the twenty-nine years I have lived in Petersburg I never before realized the gorgeousness of this part of the Hermitage." We were obliged to walk through these forbidden rooms very quietly, for fear the people in charge below would hear, and finding interlopers would probably have ejected us, if not by force, at least with a volley of Russian, which is unmusical not to say barbarous in sound. The attendant lackey seemed to enjoy giving us a glimpse of forbidden grandeur. The low wide steps of marble connected with these beautiful apartments are covered with richest velvet.

Returning through an ante-room we saw the celebrated clock in the shape of a large gold peacock with complicated works. Such a collection of snuff-boxes, some of enamel, others of gold set with precious stones. One presented by the Sultan to the wife of Nicholas I. is covered with purest diamonds, and when sent contained a shawl. Think of the texture of a shawl which could be folded and placed in a snuff-box of ordinary dimensions. Numerous cases are filled with all kinds of gorgeous bric-a-brac. I have a chaotic remembrance of ornaments of carved ivory, historical miniature dishes, of enamel toys of Catherine II., silver and gold curios from Japan

A Glimpse of the Hermitage. 145

and China, filigree ornaments, case of watches of various queer designs, bouquets of flowers formed entirely of precious stones, and the plume of Prince Potemkin, presented by a Sultan,—a mass of glittering diamonds which almost dazzle my eyes in thinking of it.

Such collections of rare articles of the greatest value we had never dreamed of, and when Pilly said, with a majestic wave of his hand: "Walk this way and behold 'ladies' delight,'" we were tempted to say: "No more, Pilly, no more." This so called "ladies' delight" was a case full of jewelled watches of artistic design and workmanship; most of them were worn as chatelaines and encrusted with gems; there must have been two hundred, and of course represented a fabulous sum. Some exquisite specimens of the lapidary's art included a walking-stick in jasper covered with diamonds, also jewelled handles for umbrellas belonging to the Empress Elizabeth. Among the numerous pocket-books are some of shell enamel, silver and gold ornamented with diamonds, and a few of the beautiful old Niello work now so rare. But I must cease; if my readers are wearied I crave indulgence; the vast museum is so wonderful that a description, however brief one may endeavor to make it, must of necessity be lengthy. Among all the wonders of this vast collection none are more beautiful than the large ornaments before referred to of the rare Siberian stones, lapis-lazuli, malachite, porphyry, jasper, and rhodonite.

Exhaustion followed our exciting morning, and we were glad to rest until six o'clock, when two American friends, residents of Petersburg, came to take us to drive before dinner. The Matron drove in a drosky with our senior host and found the national vehicle most comfortable, and although in some respects the ride was novel.

Think of a real " Rudder Grange " in Russia! Sure enough, on arriving at our host's home, we found it a house-boat, moored to Petrofsky Island, and a great improvement upon the original, only Euphemia was absent, or rather had never been present, and the German Pomona was elderly and unmusical; the novel way of living fascinated us. Rudder Grange has two stories; the salon, containing a large organ and billiard-table, is a charming room. Sunset from the deck, or veranda, whichever you choose, was fine, and the situation of Rudder Grange commands a fine view of the Neva and harbor.

Before returning to our hotel, we stopped at the Aquarium, and listened to excellent orchestral music while we drank Russian tea, wishing, meanwhile, that the delightful evening was just beginning. The sheepskin-clad moujik was lying on the door-step when we reached the Grand, and we felt a thrill of pity for those wretched men, whose duty it is to sleep all night outside the front door, all large buildings in Russia, whether public or private, being so guarded.

CHAPTER VIII.

OUR LAST DAY IN ST. PETERSBURG—SEEING THE WINTER PALACE—ON TO MOSCOW.

This chapter is likely to be a succession of adjectives, for the Winter Palace is a marvellous place, and, in its way as difficult to describe as the Hermitage. A huge building of red stucco, in which six thousand persons have lived at one time; some writer speaks of the roof having been used for colonists, who lived there with their live stock in happy confusion. The palace fronts the winter quay; in the centre is the imposing state entrance, used for balls and court festivities, and when the Emperor blesses the Neva in the winter, this entrance is thronged with officers, mighty officials, and the most exclusive of Russian nobility.

This gorgeous religious ceremonial occurs during the festival of the Epiphany, and is accompanied by chanting choirs, tapers, and incense. "The Emperor," Bayard Taylor says, "performed his part bareheaded and uncloaked in the freezing air, finishing by descending the steps of an improvised chapel and well, and drinking the water from a hole in the ice." Far and wide over the frozen surface similar holes were cut, where, during the remainder of the day, priests officiated, and thousands of the common people were baptized by immersion. As they generally came out covered with ice, warm booths were provided for them on the banks, where they thawed themselves out, rejoicing that they would now escape sickness or misfortune for a year to come. Another

Last Day in St. Petersburg. 151

very interesting ceremonial is in the spring, when, after drinking a glass of water from the Neva, the Emperor declares the river open.

The immense palace is four stories high, with a frontage of four hundred and fifty and a depth of three hundred and fifty feet. Its magnificent appointments surpassed all we had seen. The pictures, filling nine or ten galleries, are chiefly by native artists, representing Russian victories, with portraits of famous generals. In the concert and banquet-halls are gold, silver, and enamel dishes, which have been presented by different cities with bread and salt to the Tsars. There are hundreds of these superb articles, arranged on large plush brackets, covering the spaces at each end of these rooms.

The salon, decorated in white and gold, audience-chamber, rotunda, Peter the Great's throne-room, St.

George's room, and St. Nicholas Hall, vie with each other in magnificence, and are all very large. The private chapel is especially ornate. The palace also contains a church, dedicated to a particularly holy Ikon, said to have been painted by one of the Apostles. We sat for a long time in her Majesty's boudoir, and the Madame played on the cabinet piano used by the imperial lady when in the Winter Palace,—which, by the way, was rather tinny and out of tune. The private apartments of their Majesties are those used by Nicholas I. and his consort, as the reigning sovereign never uses the rooms of his immediate predecessor. The simple suite used by the late Emperor is just as he left them; in a recess is the hard camp-bed, upon which this unfortunate monarch breathed his last. The elaborately furnished apartments of the Duchess

Last Day in St. Petersburg. 153

of Edinburgh are as they were before her marriage, and we gazed at each other in the mirror which reflected her gorgeous bridal toilette; her concert grand piano was the best instrument we tried in the palaces.

Connected with these apartments is the private dining-room where the dynamite explosion took place in 1880, and but for the tardy arrival of Prince Alexander of Bulgaria, in whose honor a dinner-party was being given, the catastrophe might have been more appalling in its results. The conspirators calculated that when the bomb exploded the dinner would have just begun, but, providentially, the guest of the evening was long in making his toilette, so that it was fifteen or twenty minutes past the appointed hour when the Emperor, with his family, including the Duchess of Edinburgh, and his friends, was ready to enter the room, and at that instant the terrific explosion took place by which eleven guards on duty were mortally hurt and over fifty soldiers and servants seriously wounded. What a fearful existence must be that of the Tsar of all the Russias, never knowing when he or his loved ones will be attacked in the most dastardly manner! Surely no lasting good can come of these terrible evidences of nihilism, and granted that the abuses of Russian despotism are awful, it does not seem as if they could be righted by deeds of violence to those in authority.

The grand marble staircase and entrance impressed us to such a degree that we were obliged to sit down and gaze about, feeling ourselves lost in this immense hall. "Pilly," said the Signorina, "how does this all look when entertainments are given?" "Well, Miss," he said, "when it's all furnished, that is, lighted, carpeted, flowered, soldiered, servanted, and guarded, there's nothing like it in Europe; the uniforms of the officers and gorgeous gowns of the ladies can't be beat," and we believed him. "Come this way," he said, "and see her Imperial Majesty's *Pompeenian* bath-room," which proved to be too exquisite an apartment for use.

Connected with the white and gold salon is a large winter garden and palm-house, with an extensive aviary, and is the most enchanting spot of all. Here Catherine resorted when most wearied, and was diverted in various ways. The large garden is filled with rare plants, and the walks about it are charming. A fountain plashing and birds singing made us long to rest in the quiet spot, but there was too much to see, so on we went. In the Empress' drawing-room are pillars, mantles, vases, and candelabra of lapis-lazuli and malachite. This is one of the suite used by her Majesty when in the palace, which, however, rarely occurs. When the court is in Petersburg the Emperor usually resides in the Anitchkoff palace, on the Nevski, where he lived as Tsarevitch. In the study of Alexander II. are many gifts received by him on the twenty-fifth anniversary of his marriage—fine pictures, silver ornaments, fancy work, screens, chairs, and pillows sent from different convents, all finely embroidered. The doors of this palace are noticeable, many of buhl, others with panels of the rarest Sévres, and those of gilt, silver, and bronze are carved. On the top floor, not far from the apartment of the Grand Duke Alexis, are three large rooms filled with priceless porcelain, Sévres, and Dresden in profusion, and specimens of the rarest china and glass. We spent hours wandering about this interesting building, forgetful of lunch, packing, and notes to be cashed at the bank, for we were to leave St. Petersburg in the evening, and it was not to be expected that we would be able to tear ourselves away from the innumerable things we wished to see until we were turned out by the major-domo. The crown jewels are no longer on exhibition, being kept in a strong room on the third floor of the palace. We saw the door and the soldiers on guard, but the priceless ornaments were safely locked out of sight and reach; perhaps it was as well, as we were satiated with magnificence.

How sorry I was to leave St. Petersburg. We saw a great deal, but could have employed a month profitably in sight-seeing. The traveller going to Russia for the first time is overwhelmed at the vast treasures of every kind which have been accumulated by Peter and his successors. It seems as though in some respects Russian civilization has reached its highest point, as in no other European country has there been such enormous expenditure for works of art; then, too, she has had the inexhaustible treasures of the East to draw upon.

A procession of three droskies carried us to the station to take the 8 P.M. train for Moscow. Pilly went in advance with the luggage, and when we arrived our sleeping compartments were ready, and every thing was systematically arranged by this excellent courier. Through his management we were admitted to places that otherwise would have been closed to us; he can always be found at the Grand Hotel, and seems to be on good terms with everybody;

monks, priests, nuns, shopkeepers, major domos, lackeys, policemen, and drosky drivers seem to consider him a privileged character, and to have him for a guide was a great advantage. Our hosts of the previous evening said good-by to us after a pleasant drive on the Nevski.

We found the sleeping carriages luxurious; they are built after the style of the Mann boudoir car, but with much finer fittings, the first class being finished in mahogany and brass, upholstered in brocaded pale-blue plush; some of the compartments are for two, others accommodate four, and, being private, are to my mind preferable to the sleepers in America. In each car is a samovar, and one can have a fresh glass of Russian tea at any moment. The railroads are under the management of the government and are in excellent condition, but the long trains do not make rapid time. At the stations there is a peculiar method of letting passengers know how long the train will stop. Five minutes before leaving a gong is rung continuously, finishing with one sharp stroke ; three minutes latter this is repeated, with two taps ; this is for passengers to take their seats ; at the last moment the ring is repeated, finishing with three taps, and the train is off.

We arrived at Moscow at eleven the following morning, after a comfortable trip of fifteen hours. The country is uninteresting, being level and bare. The usual babel at the station filled us with a sense of our own helplessness, but spying a porter from the Hotel Dussaux with English letters on his cap, our troubles were over. We expected to find railway charges exorbitant in Russia, but the price for first-class tickets is not high, and second-class is of course proportionately lower. The amount of checked luggage allowed each passenger is limited, and the excess charges appalling. So one should be content with a limited supply of gowns and bonnets, or else have numerous satchels, there being an abundance of room in the compartments, and no extra charge for hand luggage. The restaurants on the Russian railroads are good, but one must be endowed with superhuman power to order a meal, as the language is impossible to experiment in; happily much of the food is placed on a large table where a choice can be indicated by signs. So no one need starve. The delicious tea is very weak, which is fortunate, as the people drink it in quantities and at all hours.

I have spoken of the railroads belonging to the government; we were told that Russia is the only country where Cook has not been able to establish a tourists' office, and no tickets can be purchased at the station until within a half hour of starting. The fare from St. Petersburg to Moscow including sleeper ticket is thirty rubles or $15.00, the distance being about four hundred miles. The road was built during the reign of Nicholas I., who ordered a line to be surveyed between the old and new capitals. The one submitted for his approval was circuitous, passing through many large towns, making the distance between eight and nine hundred miles. The Tsar was enraged, and, taking a map and a ruler, drew a straight line, saying that was to be the route, and of course his orders were obeyed, regardless of obstacles and expense.

Moscow was the capital of the vast empire until the time of Peter, who transferred the imperial residence to St. Petersburg. What disasters have overtaken the wonderful old city! Three conflagrations in the sixteenth century, the terrible plague in 1771, and finally the great sacrifice in 1812 by the Muscovites, who set fire to their beloved city sooner than have it fall into the hands of the hated French. For three days and nights the fire blazed and the inhabitants fled, taking with them as many of their belongings as they could carry. The Metropolitan took with his own hands three sacred images, the Virgins of Iberia, Vladimir, and Smolensk.

Napoleon and his army advanced to the Sparrow Hills, whence they had their first view of this Oriental-looking city, with its countless domes, spires, green roofs, and gay coloring, making a bizarre effect in the glowing sunlight. No wonder the wearied soldiers forgot their sufferings when the splendor of the city burst upon their gaze, and they felt they were to be the possessors of all the barbaric magnificence, and with renewed enthusiam they shouted: "On to Moscow! on to Moscow!" The story of the disastrous retreat of the French is well known, but I never realized the horror of the winter march until the statistics were told me;—four hundred and fifty thousand men were sacrificed in that awful campaign! How humiliating it must have been to the proud commander. When he reached Moscow and found the city deserted, he took up his residence in the Kremlin, but was obliged to flee to the Petrovski palace, two or three miles distant, until the conflagration ceased. His soldiers served him faithfully, but he basely deserted the army in its greatest need, leaving behind him compromising papers which were discovered in the pillow-slip on his iron camp-bed, now standing in the Treasury of the Kremlin.

The long drive from the station to the Hotel Dussaux, over rough pavements, through narrow streets, past innumerable *vodki* shops and dingy buildings, made us feel as if we were out of Europe. Moscow differs greatly from St. Petersburg; it is distinctly an Eastern city. The poorly dressed people seem more like Asiatics, their sheep-skin garments looking as if they had never been new, and the moujiks seemed blacker, more unkempt, and of a lower class than in St. Petersburg.

CHAPTER IX.

THE WONDERS OF THE KREMLIN.

RUSSIA is a cross between Oriental barbarism and European civilization, and Moscow represents much of the former element. There is a strange fascination about the old capital, where we found even more to see than in St. Petersburg; but I will only refer to the principal sights.

The Kremlin! Ah, it is a world in itself! The meaning of the word is not absolutely clear, but it is supposed to be of Tartar origin, signifying fortress. The walls, with five gates, are two miles in circumference, and the enclosure is crowded with churches, palaces, towers, arsenal, and treasury. Let us enter by the Redeemer's Gate, having a miraculous Ikon of our Saviour suspended above it, which French soldiers and Tartar hordes unsuccessfully endeavored to destroy. This is a holy entrance, and all men must uncover their heads when passing through the archway, and even the Emperor is expected to conform to this unwritten law.

First, to the treasury,—a huge building filled with valuable and rare objects: old armor of every description, ornamented in the most costly manner; fire-arms, standards, captured flags and colors, including those of the Streltsi, Peter's guard, who, instigated by Sophia, sister of the Tsar, revolted, but were crushed by Peter, who, with his own hand, beheaded twenty of the rebels. Notwithstanding her protestations to the contrary, Sophia was declared guilty by Peter, and incarcerated in a convent for the remainder of her days.

Some of her favorites were hanged outside the window of her cell, and the bodies left there for three months. The round room of the treasury contains a great number of crowns, thrones, orbs, sceptres, and swords. Of two superb Polish thrones, one has allegorical carving in ivory; another, presented by the Shah of Persia to Ivan the Terrible, is studded with ten thousand turquoises; but the limit of lavish expenditure is reached in the throne used by the Empress at her coronation. It is a mass of precious stones, including eight hundred and seventy-five diamonds, and twelve hundred and twenty-three rubies of the finest water. The crown of Peter is covered with rarest jewels, as are those of the kingdoms of Kazan, Astrakhan, and Siberia. The most gorgeous one, however, is that made for Peter's wife, Catherine I., which has more than twenty-five hundred diamonds, and myriads of other gems. Swords and sceptres, all studded with precious stones, made our eyes weary with their glitter; it was the same old story. We were interested in the curious double-seated throne, made for Peter and his idiotic half-brother, who was crowned jointly with him. This throne has a concealed recess behind, where the unscrupulous but brilliant Sophia used to sit, in order to prompt her brother Ivan on important occasions.

In this room are large cases, containing the coronation robes of the Tsars and Tsaritas from Catherine I. to the present reigning sovereigns. They are all elaborate, but the magnificent mantles worn at the last coronation surpass the rest. They are four yards long, of cloth of gold, bordered with ermine, and having the imperial double-headed eagle of

Russia elaborately wrought in the centre. Her Majesty's dress, of cloth of silver, with shoes of the same material, must be worth a fabulous sum. Robes of state of the Metropolitans, velvet and cloth of gold, are all gayly decorated. In a large room upstairs are many stands, filled with an enormous collection of gold and silver ornaments and household utensils of every description, not Russian only, but from all European countries,— jugs, cups, salvers, candlesticks of curious old designs, of the highest value; some superb articles having been presented by the ambassadors of the Stuart kings.

Not being satisfied with the score of palaces belonging to her, Catherine the Great planned a new one, a quarter of a mile in length, to be erected within the Kremlin, and built in the most costly manner, but she died shortly after the corner-stone was laid, and the project was abandoned. An immense model of this stands in one of the rooms. We greatly enjoyed the extensive collection of old carriages. A huge gilded one with painted panels was presented to the Tsar Boris Godunuf, by Queen Elizabeth; a miniature vehicle with mica windows was used by Peter when a child; and one belonging to the Empress Elizabeth was used as a dining-room during her journeys between Petersburg and Moscow; it accommodated twelve or fourteen people. Many others, of gilt, with painted panels, are too numerous to mention. Here also is the camp bed to which allusion was made in connection with Napoleon's base desertion of his army, and which contained the compromising papers.

The tower of Ivan is five stories high, having in each story a chime of bells, the finest being at the top.

The view from this cupola is one of the most striking in Europe; the climb is hard, and the four hundred and fifty steps seem interminable, but the reward is great. The river Moskwa, numerous buildings within the Kremlin, countless spires, towers, and minarets of silver and gold, the glorious green fields and country beyond the city boundaries, make it a matchless vision. Napoleon and his marshals saw the striking panorama from this spot, and it is not surprising that he was strengthened in his determination to own it all; but it was not to be.

The great palace is a queer conglomeration of different styles of architecture, various additions having been made. It now contains seven hundred rooms; the modern portion is a repetition of the gorgeousness we had seen elsewhere,—ball-rooms, state bedrooms and dressing-rooms, salons filled with a profusion of the rare Siberian minerals, and enormous crystal vases and candelabra from the imperial glass-works at St. Petersburg; marble rooms, halls of St. George, Alexander Nevski, St. Andrew, and St. Catherine. The latter, where the coronation drawing-room is held, has superb pillars, mantels, and tables of malachite; the inlaid floors are of finest wood, in striking designs. The large banquet-hall, where the coronation feast is held, has a dais in the centre, supporting a velvet-covered tower, on which the priceless gold and silver plate of the treasury is displayed on these brilliant occasions. The floor covering was made at different convents, in squares of a yard each, with arabesques of different colored cloth, appliquéed with gold thread, making a Moorish effect, in harmony with the superb decoration of the room. High up in the wall, opposite the imperial throne, is a broad window opening into another dining-room on the next floor for the use of the Emperor's relatives and friends, etiquette excluding all but crowned heads from the lower room. What a superb effect this room must present at the feast, with its fine ornamentation and all the lavish display of the Russian court. Four private chapels are within the palace walls, and all are elaborate in their decoration.

The most interesting apartments are those on the Terem, formerly used by the Tsaritas and their children. This antique part of the palace is four-storied, the first containing six rooms, but the number gradually diminishes until there is but one at the top. This queer place is reached by narrow, winding, carved stairs, and is over four hundred years old. The doors of iron fretwork and

The Wonders of the Kremlin. 175

the low arched ceilings are highly colored. Among the grotesque furniture is a carved bed, which belonged to the grandfather of Peter the Great, with embroidered cover worked by Peter's sister, and is hung with Chinese silks, presented three hundred years since by ambassadors from the Celestial Empire. The chapel is quite dark and nearly empty. The profuse decorations in the Terem seem to be a mixture of Moorish and Byzantine, the colors being still bright.

Standing at the foot of the famous red staircase, what reminders we had of some of the bloodiest deeds of Russian history! Now it is only used by the Emperor at his coronation, and guards are stationed at the top and bottom to prevent ordinary, every-day mortals from even putting a foot on these stairs. It was here that Ivan the Terrible committed one of his most atrocious deeds. A trusty soldier was sent with a letter from one of the leaders of his army, and while hearing the letter read the Tsar transfixed the messenger by piercing his foot with an iron-pointed staff, upon which his Majesty leaned his entire weight. Down this same stair-case was thrown the body of the false Demetrius, and during the revolt of the Streltsi many noblemen and officers were here cut in pieces by the infuriated rebels; and when Napoleon took possession of the Kremlin he proudly ascended these stairs; so, naturally, we felt a keen interest in this historic spot. Ivan did not repent of his wickedness until a short time before his death, when, taking monastic vows, he endeavored to atone for his many sins; but one cannot help being regretful that the change in his life did not occur until after he had killed his own son with a blow from his staff. His cruelty developed after the death of his dearly loved young wife, whose powerful influence had always been for good.

After seeing the palace, treasury, and tower, we were glad to rest before driving to the Sparrow Hills to dine. From the veranda of the restaurant the superb view was a revelation; a thunder-storm, followed by a rainbow shining through the haze over the picturesque city, made a charming vision. To see the Kremlin thoroughly would require weeks of constant visiting; we were forced to be content with much less time, but saw most of the churches within the walls. The Cathedral of the Assumption, where the Tsars have been crowned from the time of Ivan the Terrible, is crowded with sacred paintings, shrines, golden banners, presenting a gorgeous appearance.

In one of the small chapels are many sacred relics, among them a piece of Christ's robe, a nail of the true cross, hand of St. Andrew, and several jaws and hands of other saints. The superstitious people believe implicitly in the genuineness of these articles. Among the ecclesiastical treasures filling the sacristy is a portion of the true cross, set in a gold cross studded with diamonds, and was worn by Peter the Great at Pultava. The cathedral has five huge domes; its walls are gilded, and on the screen is hung a miraculous picture of the Virgin, covered entirely with rarest jewels, worth over a quarter of a million of dollars. In one of the silver shrines reposes the body of a priest who suffered the death penalty for his temerity in publicly reproving Ivan the Terrible for his many crimes; for which the church canonized him.

What a splendid scene the coronation must be! The description by Dean Stanley is the most interesting and complete of any I have read, and he explains many of the symbolical acts; the Emperor himself assumes the mantle, crown, and sceptre, as he is the head of the church as well as of the state.

The church in the wood is a small building not open to the public. It is one of the oldest churches in Moscow, and was built in the midst of the woods which formerly occupied a portion of the Kremlin enclosure. During Napoleon's stay in Moscow it was used as a stable, but is now restored. The Tsars are baptized and married in the Cathedral of the Annunciation, which is filled with the regulation lamps, shrines, frescos, and Ikons; the floor is noticeably beautiful, being paved with jasper and agate; but the relics in the sacristy are numerous, and seem to us almost more impossible than any others; the principal ones are a portion of the sponge on which the vinegar was offered to Christ, a portion of the crown of thorns, and a drop or two of His sacred blood. It was horrible to me to look at these highly prized treasures; there seemed to be an element of sacrilege in the idea, and yet the people firmly believe in them.

In the cathedral of the Archangel Michael are buried many of the Tsars of the Ruric and early Romanoff dynasties; the tomb of Ivan the Terrible is covered with a black pall, showing that he died a monk. One of the Ikons contains a drop of the blood of John the Baptist, which looked like a speck of ink. An object of great interest is the tomb of young Demetrius, son of Ivan the Terrible, who was torn from his watchful mother and assassinated when six

"TSAR-KOLOKOL," OR KING OF BELLS, KREMLIN, MOSCOW.

years old by order of Boris Godunuf, who became Tsar. His portrait, handkerchief, some toys, coins, bloodstained shirt, and the murderous knife by which he met his death, are all placed near his tomb, and beneath the glass top can be seen a half inch of his forehead, and scores of devotees continually kiss the spot of glass directly above the uncovered bone, or whatever it is now; it resembles a scrap of untanned leather.

Well does the "Tsar Kolokol" deserve its name "King of Bells"; it is huge, and we walked around it, sat beside it, gazed at it, and wondered at it. The figures on the outside are of the Empress Anne and Alexis. Its height is over twenty-four feet, its circumference nearly sixty-eight, and its weight two hundred tons. It stands on terra firma at the foot of the tower of Ivan, and a large piece broken out of one side stands near; its clapper, lying on the ground, looked as if it would require steam power to move it, and perhaps if rung the bell could be heard all over Europe.

The sacristy was the last place we visited in the Kremlin, and, wearied with gorgeousness, we sat on the stairs to wait for the coming of the patriarch in charge, who was lunching and would not be hurried. He was an imperious-looking man, a high church dignitary, and member of an aristocratic family, so we waited with patience. Rich sakkos, the Metropolitan's robes, fill two rooms: one, superbly embroidered, belonged to the Metropolitan Peter, who lived in 1300; another, of crimson velvet, is covered with pearls; others heavily embroidered in gold and studded with precious stones are gorgeous. But the seven mitres surpassed all in richness and beauty; four belonged to the famous patriarch Nicon, and are covered with large diamonds, rubies, emeralds, sapphires, and pearls. In this sacristy is prepared every two or three years during Lent the holy Chrism, used in baptism in the Russo-Greek Church; also the emperors are anointed with it when crowned, and it is used in the consecration of churches. It is prepared by the Metropolitan of Moscow, assisted by the highest dignitaries of the church. A large vase kept in a glass case contained the first Chrism sent to Russia from the East, on the introduction of Christianity into the empire. It is an exquisite object and made of mother-of-pearl. A few drops are taken out and a portion of the new Chrism put in, so that some of the original " sacred oil " is always there. This Chrism is composed of some thirty ingredients,—oils, spices, gums, white wine, and many other things, all made holy by the drop or two of the portion taken from the vase. An enormous silver caldron and two kettles given by Catherine II. are kept in the sacristy and into which the sacred mixture is poured when prepared; then the sixteen large silver jars presented by Paul I. are filled, and different bishops send for small portions of it when required in their dioceses. The ladles, sieves, and every thing used for making the Chrism are of sterling silver. At the baptism of children the priest crosses with a small camel's-hair brush or feather dipped in the Chrism, the mouth, eyes, ears, hands, and feet; " the eyes are anointed in order that the child may only see good, the ears that they may admit only what is pure, the mouth that he may speak as becomes a Christian, the hands that they may do no wrong, and the feet that they may tread the path of virtue "; —good theoretically, but practically impossible.

Leaving the synodal building we bowed profoundly to the dignitary in charge, who vouchsafed us the least possible acknowledgment, looking the while as though he considered us far beneath his august notice. How we longed for Pilly, who succeeded in making the most austere custodians affable.

CHAPTER X.

SIGHTS OUTSIDE THE KREMLIN— ADIEU TO RUSSIA.

ONE morning during our stay in Moscow we drove early to the Nova Devitchi Monastyr, or "New Maidens Convent," to see a procession of priests, monks, and novitiates, it being the feast day of the convent's patron saint. It was here that Sophia was imprisoned, died, and was buried, and being a long distance from the city and within high walls, she could not have had much diversion. We drove over the roughest of pavements, through narrow streets, passed great churches, some standing next dirty *vodki* shops or miserable squalid homes, and began to realize how

Sights Outside the Kremlin. 187

great an area Moscow covers. Crowds were going in our direction, some in droskies, but mostly on foot, peasants in blouses with matted hair, women with babies and children of all ages, boys with lunch in dirty paper bags,—all hurrying to keep in advance of the procession.

When within a mile of our destination, we came upon tents with tables, samovars, cups and saucers, and all kinds of untempting-looking food. There must have been accommodation for at least twenty thousand people. As our carriage could not be driven within a quarter of a mile of the gates on account of the density of the crowd, we walked with the mob, and while pushing our way to catch a glimpse of the procession, we saw enough of peasant life to satisfy us forever. Such dirt, such smells, cannot be imagined. I can see them now,—the women in ragged old frocks, with dirty kerchiefs on their heads, their coarse face unwashed, and long hair uncombed; the men in sheepskin; the children in,—well, next to nothing. Nuns were going about, and, finally, after a weary time of waiting, the procession came in sight. Among the standards carried by the men were one hundred superb golden banners belonging to the Cathedral of the Assumption, which were so heavy that their bearers were forced to rest every twenty or thirty steps.

It was impossible to find room to enter the church where service was being held, so without waiting to see the entire procession, we wended our way back to the cabs and drove to St. Saviour's, the newest of Russia's cathedrals. Erected as a thank-offering for deliverance from the French, it was proposed to build it on the summit of Sparrow Hill, the spot where Napoleon had his first view of the city, and some of the foundation was laid, when it was discovered that the sandy soil would not support the vast edifice, and the unfortunate architect was exiled to the mines of Siberia, which seems an awful injustice in these enlightened days; but the blame had to fall on some one, and this wretched man's life was blighted, and he was forever cut off from civilization and his kindred. Would this have happened in any other country? By the way, a woman whose husband is exiled to Siberia may consider herself a widow, and, if she chooses, can marry again, but some, many indeed, go with their unfortunate loved ones and share all the horrors of their sad lot. What a living death it must be! Although every one knew that the punishment of Russian offenders was severe, it has only been since the publication of Mr. Kennan's series of brilliant papers that the civilized world has been made acquainted with the appalling facts, and yet to us travelling as we did so comfortably without trouble and seeing only the bright side of every thing, it did not seem possible that these abuses could exist.

In its way, St. Saviour's is as wonderful as St. Isaac's, to which it presents a strong contrast. It is of course built in the shape of a Greek cross,—a mass of pure white marble and glittering gold dazzles one's eyes. The surrounding grounds are laid out elaborately, and flowers and shrubs were in luxuriant bloom when we saw it. Standing on quite an eminence, it can be seen from any part of the city, and has a new, fresh look, quite at variance with the other churches, and is kept scrupulously clean. Standing within the vast building, which will hold seven thousand persons, we felt ourselves lost in immensity. In the central dome is a remarkable and, to me, sacrilegious representation of the Trinity. God the Father is in the person of a benevolent-looking, elderly gentleman, the Son a beautiful child sitting upon his knee, and the Holy Ghost descending in the form of a dove. It was rather a shock to see a picture of the Almighty, and we obeyed the impulse to leave it.

The walls are covered with rare paintings by eminent Russian artists, representing different saints, patriarchs, and apostles, and, of course, Alexander Nevski. On the Ikonastas the pictures are by Neff, and on the altar are some by Verestchagin, which are remarkably fine. All the artistic work is of high merit, and worthy of careful study. The gorgeous royal stand has beautifully carved marble chairs, upholstered in cloth of gold, for the use of their Majesties; and the canopy is richly embroidered with the imperial arms. There are various Siberian minerals in pillars, floors, shrines, and candlesticks. The galleries on either side of the altar are approached by staircases, with superb gilt balustrades; the gold and enamel candlesticks are especially fine, being large and wrought in curious artistic designs. The music on Sunday was glorious, but not quite equal to St. Isaac's; that could not be expected. During the service the procession of archbishop, priests, and deacons was very imposing; clad in gorgeous robes of cloth of gold and heavily embroidered velvet, crowned with gem-studded mitres, their heavy coarse faces seemed in strange contrast.

Just outside the Kremlin stands the Cathedral of St. Basil the Beati-

CHURCH OF ST. BASIL THE BEATIFIED, MOSCOW.

Sights Outside the Kremlin. 193

fied, one of the most remarkable churches in Russia. It was erected by Ivan the Terrible, who was so delighted with the building that he ordered the architect's eyes put out, in order that he never could repeat the design. Certainly this cathedral is the most grotesque, impossible-looking building we saw. It has eleven chapels, in each of which service is annually held, in honor of the anniversary of its patron saint. It is a rambling, queer, many-corridored old place, decorated within and without in the most glaring colors. Each of the eleven chapels is surmounted by a dome, no two being of the same color or design; the architecture might be Tartar Byzantine, or, in fact, any thing. No accurate idea can be formed of its striking appearance from the accompanying uncolored illustration. Heavy chains and crosses, worn for penance by St. Basil, to whom the cathedral is dedicated, are suspended above his tomb.

The chapel dedicated to the Iberian Mother is the most holy of Russia's shrines, aud contains a miraculous Ikon of the Iberian Mother of God, brought from Mount Athos in the seventeenth century. The people believe the scar on the right cheek to be the result of a wound inflicted by an infidel, and which drew blood. On the head is a brilliant crown of diamonds and a net of rare pearls, while scattered all over the picture are gorgeous jewels. The chapel is visited daily by thousands of devotees, each leaving an offering, making the aggregate an enormous amount; much money also being earned by taking the "Mother" to visit sick people, and in a superb coach, drawn by six horses, and attended by liveried servants, the Ikon drives about in state. Whenever the

Emperor visits Moscow he drives to the Iberian chapel, and, leaving his carriage, prays for some little time before going to the Kremlin. It seems as if this must constitute a strong link between Tsar and people, for his Majesty's devotions are carried on before the sacred Ikon in the same way as those of the humblest Moujik.

Outside the Kremlin walls is the Katai Gorod, or Chinese town, having six gates. Within are many interesting buildings, the Gostonni Dvor, or Great Bazaar, being the largest, and which monopolizes most of the trade. It is an enormous building, filled with small shops and passages bewildering to strangers; the merchants are very shrewd, and, of course, ask exorbitant prices for their wares, and one needs to be very careful in making purchases. To us the shops were less attractive than in St. Petersburg, although the jeweller's work was of the best. One of our most delightful experiences in Moscow was a visit to the private picture-gallery of a wealthy merchant, whose unpronounceable name I have quite forgotten. We went with the expectation of seeing a few good pictures, but found a large gallery of eight or nine rooms filled with gems. It was there I first saw the work of that remarkably clever, versatile artist, Vasili Verestchagin. His incidents in the Russo-Turkish war filled us with horror, and certainly he paints as realistically as is possible. Our guide told us that he had incurred the Emperor's displeasure, on account of his truthful portrayal of terrible scenes during the last campaign, but I doubt the truth of the rumor, as we did not hear it corroborated by any reliable person.

A large number of charming works

by Makoffsky, the painter of the well-known "Russian Wedding" and "Choosing the Bride," represent different phases of Russian life. A St. Petersburg gamin attracted us greatly, being admirably done and full of spirit. Behind a curtain hangs a picture of Ivan the Terrible killing his own son. Not knowing what we were to see, we casually strolled towards the alcove; but in the dimness, the blood-curdling sight made us leave the locality speedily. Among the best of the collection is one of a third-class railway-carriage filled with convicts *en route* to Siberia. The train has stopped at a way-station; pigeons are picking up bits of bread thrown from the car windows by some sad, sweet-faced children, who are evidently accompanying their parents to that terrible country. Standing behind the children are the exiles, who for the moment have forgotten their misery and blighted hopes, and are amusedly watching the children's enjoyment derived from giving scraps to the birds, possibly parting with food necessary for their own nourishment. The picture is strangely pathetic, and one cannot help imagining a look of envy in the faces of the condemned ones, who, seeing the birds are free, would fain share their sense of liberty. The marine painter, Aivazofski, has great power, and the specimens of his work we had previously seen prepared us for enjoying those belonging to this gallery. "The Black Sea," a dreary stretch of angry water, fascinated us, and "A Shipwreck," with wonderful light from a rainbow, filled us with a sense of awe. Many studies and ideal heads fill two rooms; also we liked some pictures of Cairo and Alexandria. It was a most enjoyable morning, and we wandered from room to room until the hour for closing the gallery forced us to go elsewhere.

Of the Troitsa Monastery, with its twelve churches filled with priceless treasures of every description, I have not space to write ; but I must refer to the catacombs in the hermitage belonging to the monastery, filled with human beings living in total solitude, having vowed never again to look upon light of day or face of mankind. Now, what possible good can they do themselves or the world by this course ? This monastery, founded in 1342, has an enormous revenue, and is visited by over one hundred thousand devout pilgrims annually. The Simonof Monastery, several convents and museums, are all of great interest to strangers, and the longer one remains in Moscow the more one is overwhelmed at the amount of sight-seeing there is to be done. Dining at a different restaurant each evening, we found meals were very good, well served, and quite inexpensive ; most of the waiters were dressed in spotless white-linen suits. Nearly all the restaurants are provided with a large orchestrion ; some being very loud played national airs joyously.

The Romanoff House, in the Katai Gorod, gives one an accurate idea of Russian life hundreds of years since ; the interior is in the style of dwelling-houses in the sixteenth century, it having been sacked by the French and rebuilt, but the original walls remain. Michael, the founder of the Romanoff dynasty, was born here, where many of his belongings and curious souvenirs have been preserved. It is a queer, four-storied, highly decorated building ; in the basement are cellars for wine, beer, and various provisions ; the low,

ROMANOFF HOUSE, MOSCOW.

arched ceilings of the upper story are gayly colored; the doors were purposely built very low, so that ambassadors and others entering the Tsar's presence were obliged to make a profound obeisance, or failing to do this, received a blow on the head from the archway. The largest room is the royal chapel, with Gothic roof ornamented in odd devices; in the walls are many secret recesses for the concealment of treasures. An old four-post bedstead and brocade-covered benches complete the furnishings of the bed-chamber, where the ceilings and walls are of carved wood. The quaint cut of the Tsar's shirt, and Tsarita's night-dress, and the clothing worn by Michael when a child, as well as in manhood, were of great interest; but the toys in the nursery of the Terem cradles, primers and dolls, we coveted as curios; certainly a child must have longed for amusement to have been satisfied with these grotesque imitations. Some very old and valuable Ikons, much family plate of curious designs, tile stoves and writing utensils similar to those used in England in the thirteenth and fourteenth centuries, attracted our notice, and I felt as if we were far away from this prosperous nineteenth century while lingering among these quaint relics of bygone times.

The Signorina and the Madame drove to the Petrovski palace and park, three miles beyond the city limit. It was here Napoleon took refuge when the conflagration forced him to flee from the city; and before the Tsar's coronation he and his suite reside here. This is the only palace which is not crowded with ornaments, and in its plainness and simplicity it presents a striking and not agreeable contrast to the gorgeousness of the rest. The racecourse in the park is a favorite resort in summer; but the bad pavements and narrow, dirty streets did not create a favorable impression on the indefatigable sight-seers.

We spent Sunday afternoon at the Foundling Hospital, that enormous institution founded by Catherine the Great. Being August, the main building was empty, as in the summer the babies and nurses live in small cottages, of which there must be forty or fifty within the grounds. Think of fifteen hundred babies under two months old! What a harrowing sight! The day of our visit sixty had been received, and the average is fifteen thousand annually. The only questions asked are: "Has the child been baptized?" and "What is its name and age?" They are publicly brought in, their names entered in a book, and a corresponding ticket is attached to the infant; then it is carefully bathed in a copper tub lined with flannel, vaccinated, and, if perfectly healthy, sent into a ward to be given in charge of one of the buxom peasant women acting as wet-nurse, of which there are about eight hundred, wearing national costumes, with necklaces of large glass beads. Fancy one woman taking care of three screaming children of the same age. When two months old they are sent with their nurse to the country, and cared for until they become of age. If the girls marry, they receive a wedding outfit and presents of money. The boys learn trades, and some enter the army. In the hospital, many among the trained nurses were foundlings, and returned to the institution to care for other helpless creatures as they were themselves cared for.

Every thing about this vast establishment was scrupulously clean and comfortable. In the chapel there is generally baptism going on, for many of the poor infants have not been previously named. The laundry, kitchen, and every household department we found complete, but the puny babies, wailing piteously, made us heart-sick. They were swathed in muslin, with their arms bound down; the nurses let their helpless heads bob about in every direction. However, a merciful Providence removes a large percentage of them from the sorrows of this world. Some of these are children of poor but honest parents, who cannot afford to support them, and knowing they will receive excellent care send them to this hospital. The government appropriates annually an immense sum for its support, but it seems as though it must encourage crime; it is, however, a greater problem than I care to grapple with.

We expected to go to Nijni Novgorod from Moscow, but were advised by experienced friends not to undertake it, as, since the railroad facilities have increased so greatly in Russia, the fair has lost much of its Oriental character, and lacks the interest of former days. The trip is an exhausting one, so we contented ourselves with cross-questioning friends, who had found it a wearisome experience, and told us that the goods would compare favorably with those on exhibition in the Bowery, New York.

We greatly enjoyed the weeks spent in Russia; every thing seemed novel to us. In St. Petersburg and Moscow we often felt as if we were far from Europe, and the queer customs, outlandish garb of the lower classes, Oriental bazaars, and, above all, the bulb-like domes and minarets, added to the strangeness of the scene; and one great charm to me was in meeting so few tourists. "Holy Mother Moscow," with her dirt and magnificence, glorious churches and remnants of barbarism, no wonder the Russians rejoiced unspeakably at the disasters of the hated French. The gross superstition of the people, their idolatry and devotion to outward forms and to their Ikons, are alike strange and repulsive. In the cathedrals, the priceless jewels, splendid pictures, ornaments of rarest minerals, the lavish expenditure on the smallest details, were in strange contrast to the poor, squalid, ignorant people thronging the churches, whose rapt devotion was remarkable. In the numerous palaces, ornaments, and furnishings the wealth of the Tsar is shown; his power is supreme, his possessions past computing, and always increasing.

Russia impressed me as too vast to comprehend; figures convey but small idea to one's mind, but her territory equals one half of Europe, and her undeveloped resources and wealth are enormous, and far exceeding our comprehension. What the future will be of this wonderful country no one can predict, but at all events Russia would be a most dangerous and mighty foe. Her army is immense, and if the wealth of jewels, rare minerals, and priceless ornaments of all kinds were converted into rubles, it seems as if her power would be limitless. Then, too, what might she not accomplish in educating the masses of the people, if the vast sums were expended in that way, instead of in decorating palaces and churches. The amount represented in jewels alone would be sufficient to raise from degradation millions of ignorant, superstitious peasants, whose enlightenment is less than that of the heathen, but most of whom are strangely patriotic.

But amid all these splendors, my mind constantly reverted to the days spent in tranquil, picturesque Norway. There can be no lovelier country on earth, and away in those northern waters we felt the power and majesty of God to a profound degree.

Fair Poland, how sad a fate is thine! From Moscow we went directly to Warsaw. The trip was fatiguing, and in spite of a comfortable railway carriage the forty hours seemed interminable. From the Prague suburb of the city, we drove to the extensive Hotel d'Europe, where the management and food are Russian. A national soup we experimented upon had a block of ice floating in the remarkable decoction, of which a taste more than sufficed.

The royal castle stands in a square near the hotel, but most of its treasures have been carried to St. Petersburg and Moscow. We took long walks past monuments, shops, and churches, which, after the splendor of Russia's cathedrals, looked plain to us. The beautiful Saxony garden, with fine fountains, lovely flowers, and a labyrinth of paths, stands in the centre of the town, and is the citizens' favorite resort.

From the cupola of a Lutheran church we had an excellent view of Warsaw; the city covers an enormous space, but failed to impress us favorably. Driving in the park was our only diversion. The pavements were rough, and many buildings seemed to be falling into decay. Stationed in the streets were mounted Russian guards, and everywhere we saw evidences of a conquered country, and an air of neglect seemed to pervade the city. There are, however, some fine private residences, standing in the midst of extensive grounds, belonging to noble Polish families. While driving we saw a few beautiful women, but being summer most of the upper classes were out of town. Reflecting upon the present condition of Poland filled us with sadness. How bravely her sons fought to preserve their liberty and rights; how many names are enrolled among the noblest of patriots, but their bravery and sacrifices were in vain, and to-day this fair country is divided between Russia, Prussia, and Austria. The Polish refugees we have met in America have shown such nobility and grandeur of character that we have longed for an extensive acquaintance among their country people. Our stay in Warsaw depressed us, and we felt a righteous indignation against those who conquered these brave patriotic people.

We spent pleasant days in Berlin, where many military reviews held by the Kaiser, museums, galleries, beautiful parks, fine shops, and advanced civilization were quite to our taste. In Dresden, with its deservedly famous picture-galleries, and superb representations of Wagnerian operas, our enjoyment was great.

From thence we went to Cologne, with its traditional smells, grand cathedral, and church of eleven thousand virgins, where the bones of the slaughtered maidens are arranged on the walls in grotesque designs. To the Cologne gallery belongs Richter's ideal portrait of the adored Queen Louisa, from which we could not tear ourselves, and after a prolonged view returned again and again to gaze spellbound on the exquisite face and figure so beautifully portrayed.

Down the Rhine we went to Bingen where the mouse tower and restored feudal castle of Rhinestein vie with each other in picturesque beauty, and from there to bright, beautiful Paris, the American Mecca.

www.ingramcontent.com/pod-product-compliance
Lightning Source LLC
Chambersburg PA
CBHW021803230426
43669CB00008B/614